Shipping Container Homes

How to Build a Homemade and Eco-friendly Living

(Avoid Daily Stress and Live in Your Dream Home With Your Family)

Harold Willis

Published By **Regina Loviusher**

Harold Willis

All Rights Reserved

Shipping Container Homes: How to Build a Homemade and Eco-friendly Living (Avoid Daily Stress and Live in Your Dream Home With Your Family)

ISBN 978-1-77485-561-4

No part of this guidebook shall be reproduced in any form without permission in writing from the publisher except in the case of brief quotations embodied in critical articles or reviews.

Legal & Disclaimer

The information contained in this ebook is not designed to replace or take the place of any form of medicine or professional medical advice. The information in this ebook has been provided for educational & entertainment purposes only.

The information contained in this book has been compiled from sources deemed reliable, and it is accurate to the best of the Author's knowledge; however, the Author cannot guarantee its accuracy and validity and cannot be held liable for any errors or omissions. Changes are periodically made to this book. You must consult your doctor or get professional medical advice before using any of the suggested remedies, techniques, or information in this book.

Upon using the information contained in this book, you agree to hold harmless the Author from and against any damages, costs, and expenses, including any legal fees potentially resulting from the application of any of the information provided by this guide. This disclaimer applies to any damages or injury caused by the use and application, whether directly or indirectly, of any advice or information presented, whether for breach of contract, tort, negligence, personal injury, criminal intent, or under any other cause of action.

You agree to accept all risks of using the information presented inside this book. You need to consult a professional medical practitioner in order to ensure you are both able and healthy enough to participate in this program.

Table of contents

Introduction 1

Chapter 1: Does The Shipping Container Make A Good Home? 10

Chapter 2: Choosing The Right Container For You 23

Chapter 3: Sorting Out The Legal Matters 38

Chapter 4: Doing The Foundation (Literally) 55

Chapter 5: Buying The Container 68

Chapter 6: The Interiors: Putting Them In Place 82

Chapter 7. 7 Benefits Of Home Design For Shipping Containers 103

Chapter 8: The Shipping Container Pros And Pros And 110

Chapter 9: How To Build The Home Of A Container 125

Chapter 10: Design Your Shipping Container Home 134

Chapter 11: Ideas Of Home Plans Design Your Home 144

Chapter 12: Preparation Of The Site 163

Chapter 13: Foundations: Types 173

Chapter 14: Things To Keep In Mind When Building A Shipping Container Home ... 179

Introduction

Many of you may not have thought of the origins of shipping containers. They are not important to most people's daily lives. We live in our cities and towns, so shipping containers are just what we see at ports or on cargo ships. Most people have never seen a container in real life, except for the occasional Hollywood action with the containers hidden in the background. Imagine if I said that one of those containers could make a huge difference in your life.

Port of Los Angeles (CA, USA)

Malcolm McLean created the first shipping container in the 1950s. This simple invention would revolutionize transportation. Even those who believe they have nothing to do the large metal beasts have probably used or bought something shipped in these containers. This might seem like it isn't as important as I said. It is, in a sense. But there's more.

These massive boxes were used by the U.S. Military to supply its troops during the Vietnam War. They also found a new use for them. They began using them as emergency shelters. The shipping container home trend has been going strong for many years and is only getting stronger.

A shipping container home is a great option for someone tired of paying rent, mortgages, and loans.

The Cost Problem

It is becoming more difficult to buy a house. CNBC's Baldwin report, 2021, shows that home prices have risen 13.2% since 2020 and that 20.5% fewer homeowners are willing to sell their homes. This suggests that although there is an increase in demand for homes, the supply of these properties may not be growing at the same pace. The gap between supply and demand has always contributed to higher prices. The cost of buying a home in the United States can be quite expensive. Prices range from USD $149,000 to USD $730,000, depending on where you live. The lower price is for an average home in Arkansas, while the higher price is for a typical Hawaii home. However, the average home costs USD 375,000 today (Fontinelle 2020).

These numbers can be intimidating, especially for first-time homebuyers looking to find a place to raise their children or grandchildren. There have been always been segments of society that have been drawn to cheaper homes, such as retirees and new families. However, because of rising housing prices, shipping containers homes are now at an interesting transition point, where professionals with steady incomes are choosing these living spaces. You may be asking, "Why?" The mortgage is the short answer.

Mortgages can be a long-term commitment and quite costly. It doesn't take long to see statistics that show that getting a mortgage is becoming more difficult. White, 2020. A recent NBC news report mentioned how Wells Fargo and JPMorgan Chase have increased their credit standards to 700 and 720 respectively. The typical young professional wants to live a life that is not financially restrictive. This financial need is perfectly met by shipping containers. Shipping containers are a growing market. This book is a sign that you are serious about owning your dream home. This is exactly what this book will help you do. Let's first understand why shipping containers are such an attractive housing option.

Shipping Container Homes: Why?

Did you know that these containers are only used once in their lives before being melted down and remodeled into another container? Because of their huge structure, shipping them back to where they came from is difficult. It is financially and logistically most feasible to just let them rest at ports until they can be used again. They could be used for beautiful, affordable homes or new-age workspaces.

WineBox Valparaiso Container hotel in Chile

Shipping container homes are not only convenient. Shipping containers have much more to offer than convenience. Shipping containers offer many advantages, not only the unique style that they can be transformed into, but also many other benefits that make them an attractive option for most people.

Cheap: These containers can be purchased at a low price. A brand-new container can be purchased for USD $7,000 but a used container may be available for USD $3,300. The cost of building the container into a home will cost you between USD $30,000 and $40,000. This is less than the average Arkansas housing cost. We have not yet considered the cost of adding two or more structures to the mix, as well as interior design. However, the shipping container home price is unbeatable even with these additional costs.

Sturdy: Shipping containers can withstand harsh weather conditions at sea without causing damage to the goods inside. These boxes are strong and durable. They provide protection from storms, hurricanes and other weather conditions. However, they can also withstand the harsh glares of the sun because they are made of weathering steel (also known as Corten Steel). This alloy helps to protect the structures against rusting and contributes greatly to their safety.

Available: There are always stacks of empty shipping containers in ports cities. If you live in one, you may find them more easily. You can get great deals at the local level and the ports would love to take them off your hands. This doesn't mean you won't have access to the containers even if your home is not in a port. It simply means that you will have to pay more for transportation to get the container to your site.

Eco-friendly: As global climate crisis continues to grow, people are more conscious of their carbon footprint on the planet. Even environmentalists are advocating for the repurposing of shipping containers that have been left at ports. It is much more energy-efficient to reuse them than to build new homes. This is not for second-hand containers. However, it is worth considering the environmental impact of new containers.

Flexibility in design: Shipping containers can be stack up in many ways, both horizontally and vertically to create some really unique designs. You can also use the same containers to create traditional, formal architecture. They are popular with a broad range of consumers who have different interests.

It takes very little time to build these homes. It is tedious and complex to build a home from scratch. It is not uncommon to find a property that is ready for you to move in, even if it has been purchased. Shipping container homes offer a unique opportunity for people to live in their own shipping containers without the need to wait years, months, or even weeks. Shipping container homes can be built in days if the conditions are right.

The Good, the Bad, and the Ugly

I understand what you are thinking. It sounds too good to be true. There is, however, a downside to this. There are always drawbacks to shipping containers. There are usually workarounds. These are important to know so that your container is safe when it arrives at its destination.

Rust: These containers are made from Corten Steel, which is resistant to rusting at deep levels. This is true even if the shipping containers are traveling across oceans. However, rust may seep into the containers more easily as the climate changes and the containers are still on the ground at the port. Shipping containers can last for almost 100 years, but when you build a home, this is something you cannot do. The problem cannot be solved by simply painting. You must sandblast the container and then recoat it.

Toxic substances It could contain biohazards, toxic substances, or other harmful substances. If you intend to live in the structure for a prolonged period of time, this could prove dangerous. Even small amounts of these substances can pose a danger.

Temperatures: We mentioned earlier that shipping containers are sun-resistant. They protect the inner material from the sun's glare, but they don't resist heat. Steel is a good conductor. This can lead to heat trapped in the container, which could cause your home to get very hot. Insulating the container is a cost-intensive option to prevent this from happening.

People tend to look at the downsides of shipping container homes when comparing them to the benefits. These risks must be managed properly so that they don't compromise your health or the health of your loved ones.

Chapter 1: Does the Shipping Container Make a Good Home?

We all know that houses and homes are different. Homes are much more than just a building. They can also inspire feelings of warmth and love. Homes are an integral part of the life journey that we choose to embark on. It is not an easy decision to make about the future of where you will live. The decision to purchase a home is an intimate and personal choice. This decision requires a lot of thought and discussion with yourself as well as your family. Even though shipping containers are the most affordable housing option, it will require a lot of consideration. You will be spending a significant part of your life in this home, but you will also make memories that you'll cherish for the rest of your life.

A shipping container may not evoke the same feeling of "home" as a traditional home when you first see it. This is because most people's mental picture of a shipping container home might be one that looks rough, metallic, or rusted. That is a living space!

Most likely, not! A rusty, old container is not something anyone would like to live in. This is not what a shipping container home looks like. Containers used are in excellent condition and as good as new. They have been used very rarely, even though they were built to last for hundreds of years.

You can't believe that most people are still hesitant to live in a shipping container. It will be comfortable. Is it safe? It will look great. Many things are often on people's minds when I talk to them about shipping container houses. Would it be possible to answer all these questions with a loud, affirmative "yes"? This is a picture of the Urban Rigger from Copenhagen.

Urban Rigger, Copenhagen

It doesn't look as uncomfortable, dangerous, or ugly as you might expect. The structure was constructed in 2016 to support the growing number of students who moved to the area. Although you can only see two sides of this house in the photo above, it is actually triangular with one container that has solar panels fitted to the top. This provides electricity for the house.

The Industrial Look

These are modern shipping container homes. They are sleek, industrial, and stylish. They can be furnished inside just like a regular house. This is why shipping container homes are becoming more popular. I hope you're starting to feel excited about all the possibilities shipping container homes could open up for your family. You are ready to get started and learn more about what you should consider before you build your container home.

Safety

Safety is one of the main concerns when shipping containers are considered as housing options. These containers are safe? There are two components to safety considerations. The first is structural integrity. The second, which applies to containers that have been used, concerns toxic substances. Let's examine these two issues in greater detail.

Structural integrity simply means that containers can be used safely even in conditions that are not recommended. The containers can still function well even in adverse conditions. Many people argue that shipping containers should be stacked side-by-side, but that when they are used in unusual designs that require stacking in random ways, it can compromise their structural integrity. The integrity of the container is further compromised every time you drill into it or use a saw to cut out windows or doors.

This argument is valid. However, it should be noted that structural modifications must be made with enough care to ensure the structure can withstand the load. Shipping containers are extremely strong structures. Shipping containers are extremely strong and can withstand natural disasters, both when they cross oceans and when they are used for architecture on the ground. There are many resources on the internet that explain how these homes have survived disasters such as earthquakes and storms. Hopefully, you can now forget any concerns about the safety of your shipping container home.

Next, toxic substances. This is a serious concern for second-hand containers, as I have already
mentioned. Unfortunately, there is no way of knowing for certain where the container has been or what it has carried. Although I will discuss how to find the container's history in the book, it is not a guarantee. Containers may have carried anything, from biohazards to pesticides and fumigants. These toxins could have leaked into the container because oceans can be turbulent. These toxins are often absorbed by the container's surfaces, making them even more dangerous.

This is something that can be overcome. Later, I will discuss how to make sure that the containers are not contaminated with chemicals. The best solution is to simply use a new container brought directly from the manufacturer unit. Although experts recommend that new containers are used to avoid any complications, some people prefer to use second-hand containers due to budget constraints or the desire for being more eco-friendly.

A crucial thing to note is that whether you are buying an old container or a new one, it will have had exposure to chemicals--second-hand containers could have more due to the transportation of chemicals, but even new containers may have their wooden floors treated with pesticides unless the company is specified not to when you order. Even though the chemicals are very small, they can still pose a problem if you and your family live with them for long periods of time.

These safety issues are not meant to scare you, but to help you be aware of the things that you should consider when building a container as your home. These problems can be addressed while the container is being built. This is how most homes are constructed.

Local Regulations

When researching before building your home, it is important to consider housing regulations. This applies to any type of housing plan, not just shipping containers. These regulations can be confusing and overwhelming for many people. It can be difficult to go to the local zoning offices and get the permits you need. These regulations are mandatory for all homeowners. No matter how much money was spent, a building can be legally demolished if it violates any local regulations.

We've established that it is exhausting to get permits for a home and a thorough understanding of the regulations. Let's add "shipping container homes" just for fun. What happens when you tell the zoning officer that you want to build a shipping container house for yourself? To be honest, he may not understand what you are saying. This is not a good place to put your container home dreams!

Shipping containers homes will likely have to go through more hurdles than regular home designs in terms of regulations regarding design and foundation. Container home builders face a problem because the concept is still relatively new. There isn't much information available about the details of these homes. When you tell someone that you would like to build a container house, they could imagine anything, from a cramped, restricted box to an imaginative structure inspired by abstract art. Understanding local regulations is crucial for homeowners who are shipping containers. These regulations can vary based on where you live. Chapter three will discuss the regulations in more detail. For now, I would say you should begin researching them and becoming familiar with them before doing anything else.

Expenses

Shipping container homes are distinguished from traditional houses by their cost. This is something we've already discussed. The best reason to consider shipping container homes is the low cost. Shipping container homes offer homeowners an affordable upfront cost for buying a home. However, there are costs specific to shipping containers.

Many people forget to create a budget. Many people get so excited about building their home, they have no idea how much it will cost. You will likely find yourself in a difficult situation if you don't do your research. You don't want that to happen. This is an important step in the future. It is worth taking the time to learn more about it.

We aren't necessarily trying to find exact numbers when we talk about budgeting. These numbers may vary depending on the design of your container home. It is essential to understand the approximate cost of each item. Consider the following factors when estimating your budget.

Insulation: This is the most expensive expense you'll incur. Steel is a good conductor for heat. This means that when it's warm outside, much of the heat will be carried into your home via the container walls. The interior of a container home may feel more like a furnace if you live in a warm environment. It can also feel like you're at the North Pole when winters are cold. Insulation of container homes is a necessity most of the year. This is also why budgeting should take into account.

It is important to consider the location. The construction process will be affected by the location of your land. Some geographical features are better suited for building containers homes than others. It is easier to build containers homes on flat land. However, if the land slopes, it will require more excavation, which in turn would increase the cost.

Permits cost money: They also impose specific requirements on construction to ensure safety for the occupants. These codes are known as building codes. They are specific to each state or region.

Amenities: Shipping container homes come in many designs, as we have already mentioned. When budgeting, it is important to consider the cost of furniture and fittings. This would include fixtures for your bathroom, bedrooms, living area, kitchen, garage, or any other space you may need. Your cost estimates can be influenced by the quality and finish you choose.

Utilities include water, plumbing and electrical wiring. If you live in an area with a lot of infrastructure, the municipality will provide water and electricity. Even so, connecting them to an unusual structure such as a shipping container home may require skilled labor that is more expensive than manual labor. If you live in an area that is not under municipal jurisdiction, you may need to find creative solutions to water, electricity and sewer problems. Bore-wells, solar panels, and septic tanks might be able to fix some things, but they are also more expensive and time-intensive than other options.

Labor: Many people are interested in building their shipping container homes themselves. It can be rewarding and enjoyable. It is best to hire a professional if you have no construction experience. This can add up to a significant cost. Even if your goal is to do it yourself, it's likely that you will need assistance.

Container-related expenses: In addition to the actual cost of the container, which depends on its size and whether or not it is brand new, you also have to consider the logistical costs involved in transporting the container from your site to where you intend to build. This cost can vary depending on how far you live from either the port for a used container or the factory for a new container. These containers are difficult to transport and require specialized equipment to lift them and place them. This is an expense that many people forget to consider. Another cost to be aware of is the removal of toxic chemicals from the container.

This is only one method of getting an estimate on your cost. This is the bottom-up approach because you build a cost estimate by looking at the prices of its components. There are many other approaches to budgeting. Another way to approach a budget is to simply take an estimate based on, for example, the cost of shipping a friend's container home and adjust upwards or downwards depending on how different it differs from what you plan. This is not always the best way to go, as there are many moving parts to the equation. It might prove difficult for an individual to account for these factors (as opposed large organizations with more resources).

After you've done your research, you'll be able to make an informed decision on whether this is the right thing for you. This information will allow you to have informed conversations with your family about the major shift you are making. Living in a shipping container home does not mean you can live in a traditional house. The lifestyle is so different that it is sometimes referred to as tiny house living. This is essentially because of the minimal space requirements.

A shipping container home does not have to be tiny. Although the containers can be stacked together to make mansions, a basic shipping container house is still smaller than some people are used to. It is important to ensure that you and your family are financially, emotionally, as well as physically, and spatially, ready for the move.

It tells me that you are committed to this endeavor for the long-term by continuing to read it. It's now time to find the right container for you.

Chapter 2: Choosing the right container for you

Container shipping structures have found a home in many sectors. The part you see here is Common Ground, South Korea's first and largest container shopping mall. It is made from 200 blue shipping containers just like the one shown in the photo.

South Korea: Common Ground

Many people around the world have discovered amazing ways to use these containers to create stunning, interesting, and most importantly efficient designs. As you look through more designs, you'll see that there are many options for the types of containers used. It is easy to end up with something more than you need or not sufficient for your needs if you don't know about these variations. We will be discussing how to choose the right container for your needs in this chapter.

Things to Consider

You might be interested in learning a few technical details. It can be difficult to remember all the dimensions and costs if you don't have any construction experience. This information is important to have on hand when you plan your home's layout and budget calculations.

Types of containers

Many containers are available that can be used for different industrial purposes. These containers can also be used creatively to build your container home. Let's take a quick look at the different types of containers available and see how they can be used in your home design.

Standard containers/dry containers: These containers are the most commonly used in the industry. These containers are also known as general-purpose containers. They can be sized up to 40 feet in length. Because of their closed, rigid structure made of Corten

Steel (which we have already discussed), they are completely protected from the elements. These containers are used in the majority of shipping container designs.

High-cube containers are identical to standard containers, except for their height. Standard containers measure 8.6 feet high, while high-cube containers stand at a foot taller. These containers are often preferred to standard containers because they offer more insulation and height without compromising the intended height.

Vented containers: Because they have specialized vents, these containers are less frequently used. These vents can be useful for transporting materials susceptible to condensation such as dry grains and coffee beans. These vents provide passive airflow which maintains dryness and reduces the likelihood of spoilage. Although they are not ideal for shipping containers homes, I am mentioning them here because of the many creative uses they have seen over the years. These containers were previously used in supply chains by Starbucks to create chic, stylish drive-thru stores across the United

States. The possibilities are limitless when it comes to shipping container architecture.

Containers with an open top The containers described above are different from other containers in that they feature a convertible or open top. They can be used to store materials that require top-loading using cranes. For example they can make it simpler to lift large granite blocks by lifting them from top. Because a top that is removable could compromise the structural integrity in a significant way and cause damage to the structure, they are typically strengthened from all sides to ensure that the structure can maintain its solid shape, even when it must carry the load in every direction. These containers are perfect when you are thinking of building an edifice with multiple floors or an additional roof. They can help you avoid the hassle of cutting off the roof of a container. When designing take into consideration the vitality of the strength of the structure. It is best to talk to an engineer who can help you make sure that you're not putting your safety at risk by your structure.

Double-door tunnels The containers are can be opened on both sides, giving them a an appearance of a tunnel. They allow loading of the container much quicker since they can be loaded on both sides. Double-door containers are perfect for commercial stores with double-bunked construction with an opening between them.

Storage containers with an open side They are open only the one hand (length-wise). These containers are ideal because they are more accessible loading and unloading are significantly less hassle. Containers with an open side are great for those who want to put in full-height windows. Doors can be left open since they are used for the purpose of security in the event that you need to secure and leave your house.

Containers that are insulated and reefers The term reefer is also known as a refrigerated container. Containers that are insulated and reefers provide temperatures control within the container by using an external power source as well as the coating of an insulation material or. Although they may appear to be an attractive alternative to an ordinary container that avoids the process of insulation however, there are a few disadvantages that make them less suitable for use. To make them habitable, they require the cutting of their sides to create windows and doors and, with an additional coating of insulation it can turn into a tedious task. There are also disadvantages, such as the space being less than standard containers, and a greater chance that the insulation could be ignited when welding process begins. Overall, buying a normal container then insulate it in the traditional method is a cheaper job.

Half-height containers: They are especially attractive. As the name implies smaller than normal containers. They are believed to have a lower center of gravity and could therefore be used to transport large and heavy cargo. Since they're already constructed to withstand the weight of heavy loads they don't require any more reinforcement. A Australian company named Shipping Container Pools is already designing these stunning containers that are half height.

Containers made of flat-racks are containers with only two walls on the shorter side of the container. They are typically used to transport specific cargo that is oversized. They are, however, rarely used for construction. They're definitely NOT recommended to be used for the primary construction, however they can be helpful when the construction of a balcony or deck which is attached to the main home.

If you are considering the various types of containers to use in your design concepts for your home It is vital to seek out professional assistance to make sure that the structural integrity is maintained of your house. Remember, your home is where you're supposed to feel safe and secure. Keep in mind that even though they can be all creatively utilized in your homes but the two first ones, i.e. dry containers that are standard and high-cube ones, are the most popular and well-known containers for homes built with containers. In the following sections, we'll discuss things to keep in mind when thinking concerning the two.

The size of the container

In a conventional home, you are in complete control of determining the dimensions and size of a space but shipping containers don't provide the same degree of freedom. As mentioned above dry standard containers come with measurements of or 40 feet in length, 8 feet in width and 8.6 feet in height. High-cube containers have identical dimensions but they measure 9.6 feet tall. The two areas in which you can have some flexibility are the length and height.

Be aware that the size of the container doesn't need to be as big as your house. 20-foot containers are usually adequate for only one or two persons. The more people in your home the larger space you'll definitely require. In the event of more than two people then a 40-footer will probably serve you better. But don't worry in case that 40 feet isn't enough. It is possible to add more containers vertically as well as vertically, according to your preferences. Be sure that the containers are of the identical size, as even minor differences can cause problems when joining two containers.

The most important thing to consider however, is the height. A single foot might seem like a small issue, but keep in mind that shipping containers can be uncomfortable if you're used to living in larger areas, and a single foot can change the atmosphere. This is particularly relevant when insulation is part of the scene.

But since high-cube containers rarely are employed in transport therefore, they won't serve the goal of being environmentally friendly since you may need to purchase one from a manufacturer. Additionally, they can be more expensive not just in relation to the container, but in terms of transport as well. Since they weigh more and larger, they require specially-designed transportation vehicles. However, in spite of these aspects these are the best options for homes built in containers since it's not often that you construct a house and you may like to build it in a perfect way.

Freight Trucks are used to
Transportation of Shipping Containers

Costs are involved

Although homes built with shipping containers win the affordability race hand-in-hand but it's still important to be aware of the cost of construction. Many people are surprised when they realize it is the container isn't the only expense they'll be paying for. There are many other expenses to consider within your spending plan, which is discussed in. In this particular section however, we'll concentrate on the costs which are associated with the containers themselves.

Prices for shipping containers have been affected by the COVID-19 virus. The current situation is causing a shortage of container which is why it is now going to cost more money to purchase containers than it would had been prior to 2020. A brand new 20-foot. container was priced between USD $2,000 to $5,000, they be priced between USD $5,000 to $6,000. A 40-footer which would cost between USD

$5,500 and $2,500 can't be purchased for less than USD $6,500, and could cost upwards of USD $7,500. Containers that are used have been sold at similar costs. A used 20-footer can cost you approximately USD $2500 while used 40 footers can cost as high as USD $3,300.

If you're thinking about the causes of the price variations Three major elements influence the cost that are the condition of the vessel, the severity of damage, as well as the past history of repairs. So, if you're buying a brand new container for a very cheap price, you may need to dig deeper at the above-mentioned aspects as well.

When you have analyzed the price of the container it is important to consider additional expenses. The primary expense is as we mentioned previously, the expense of transport. A second major expense is the cost of insulation along with the cost of labor. Costs for labor will, of course, be reduced significantly when you have previous prior experience in construction and are able to perform the refurbishing part by yourself. The cost of insulation materials is, however, not reduced. Be sure to have the most efficient plumbing and accessories. Keep in mind that I mentioned the best, not necessarily the most expensive. By investing in furniture of the highest quality now, you can save you lots of discomfort in the future. Keep in mind that shipping containers aren't designed to be lived in. They undergo several chemical treatments and get floorings treated using pesticides. They have to be meticulously cleaned and modified so that they can be used. If you are not willing to undergo the process, you can purchase containers that have already been cleaned and altered.

If you'd like assistance with the construction process, there are companies who will help you renovate your homes from beginning to end. Of course, it is going to cost you money but you can count on the highest quality of work when you work with these companies. In addition, when you are working with the same group of people since day one it's easier to ensure everyone is on the same page regarding the things you want your home to look similar to.

Prefabricated Shipping Container Homes

The range of people who would like living in containers homes is extensive. There are those who prefer to construct their own home using themselves. They're adept with equipment and work, and find the process of building very satisfying. There are people who are intrigued by the concept that they could live in containers but haven't thought about the amount of work that is involved. They are apprehensive about the whole process and the technical details could slow their enthusiasm down very quickly. If you are in the second group then there's an option that is better for you: prefabricated containers for shipping homes.

Custom-designed prefabricated container homes

Container homes that are ready to live in are developed by design firms and can be purchased through the internet. They are able to be customized according to the needs of the buyer and delivered directly to the consumer. One of the major advantages of these manufactured shipping container homes is that they have been constructed in accordance with the regulations of the zoning regulations , which makes it a less stress for homeowners. In addition, these manufacturers are able to offer assistance in the actual construction of the home.

Shipping container homes made of prefabricated materials come in different designs, ranging starting with basic designs that can cost you about USD $15,000 to larger and more sophisticated extravagant designs that cost USD $500,000 and more. They can deliver your container home to you in 10 weeks or less. Many people love the idea that they can build their own home, constructed according to their requirements without having to worry about building anything independently. These prefabricated shipping container houses can be more comfortable and cost-effective, modern or traditional, based on the needs of your family.

Once you've been taught the fundamental information you'll require now it's time to go to the next chapter within this text.

Chapter 3: Sorting out the Legal Matters

Although shipping container homes can be but they aren't permitted to be constructed everywhere. Each country has its own set of regulations and rules to be adhered to. This would be the reason that the container homes of different countries across the globe are alike. Although this variety opens many possibilities for homeowners to play around with the design in many methods, it generates an atmosphere of uncertainty.

If someone tells you they would like to construct an apartment in a shipping container, one might think that they are building something simple. However, as we've seen containers do not need to be simple in any way. Imagine telling your friends you're going to get a cat, and then you decided to get the tiger! It's true that it's an animal family but it's very unlikely that people believed that you'd be getting an animal. For container homes there is a lack of uniformity that could be a problem. Container homes can trigger many questions to the mind of municipal officials and this uncertainty can not be for your benefit.

This is that it is essential to be as prepared as you can to deal with any questions or concerns from the authorities. It is vital to be aware of exactly what you're seeking, what laws of the state say regarding it, and what the possible questions could be asked.

Researching your Location Options

As homes built using shipping containers increase in popularity, a number of nations have had to revise their construction laws. Today, many countries such as those of the United States, Denmark, New Zealand, France, Indonesia, Chile, Bangladesh, Australia, Spain, Uganda, Vietnam, and England permit the construction of homes made from shipping containers. There are many other countries who are on the way to explore this possibility more deeply than they did before. However, keep in mind that, even within these nations containers homes might not be accepted in every region.

If, for instance, you're building in the UK then you'll need the permission to plan (the approval required for any type of construction by the municipal authorities) only if you are using several containers included in your plan. A single container is deemed to be temporary housing, and thus doesn't require permission, so to speak. Similar is the case for New Zealand, but some cities will only permit the use of the home of a single container with wheels.

If you live somewhere in the United States, most states permit the construction of container homes. This allows for the construction of shipping containers. It has two additional benefits in these states aside from the obvious environmental advantage. First, the tiny homes are an effective solution to the problem of homelessness as well as being more economical. Another reason is that containers are a symbol of everything modern, from their minimalist design to their low cost, government sees the opportunity for them to support and promote unconventional investment into their economy, in the form of malls, hotels, container hotels and more. It is true that it makes the government appear as if they are growing along with new trends?

The states include Florida, Texas, Georgia, Pennsylvania, New York, Oregon, Missouri, Alaska, Washington DC, Minnesota, Tennessee, North Carolina, Colorado, California and Louisiana For instance, these states permit the construction of homes built using shipping containers currently. Although some states have a few rules to follow, other states may require that you adhere to specific rules more rigorously. Many states that do not have laws specifically governing home shipping containers are in the process of implementing these rules. The industry of shipping container homes is expanding and everyone wants to join in.

Naturally, the rules are less and less the further you travel from counties and towns. However, it is a disadvantage that it becomes harder to access services such as electricity, water supermarkets, gas and the list goes on. Connectivity to the internet and phones could be another issue in these situations.

Monitoring the Neighborhood

If you've settled on an area that is large you want to purchase, be aware of certain aspects before purchasing the property. Many who would like to reside in a shipping container house opt for living a simple life. It is because a majority of them are drawn to having the option of moving bit away from the bustle of cities and to a remote rural region. Of course, this is however, not the case for all homeowners of container homes. Certain shipping containers can be constructed directly within populated areas, provided local regulations permit it. The distinction between urban and rural settings for a home built in a shipping container is that the urban setting offers the most flexibility regarding what can be permitted, it also offers you a solid framework with regards to accessibility and amenities. Therefore you can think of it as an exchange between design freedoms and the amenities of living. Many people seek an equilibrium that allows them to get the most of both.

If you opt to build a container house "off-the-grid," there are certain things you'll consider observing within your community. One of them is the accessibility the property. If the property you're buying is remote enough that it is not connected to any road the process of accessing your property could be a challenge. If you must get to your property via the property of someone else, for instance it is necessary to obtain the permission of their written consent to do this. In most cases, easements can be granted on a basis of mutual understanding however, remember that the other party isn't legally bound to grant permission to pass over their properties. So, once you've reached an agreement it is crucial that this clause is included in the agreement for purchase and sale of the land you own. A similar agreement would have been reached for pipelines, cables and other utilities fixtures.

Another aspect of rural life that is often overlooked is the resource agreements. There is a common misconception that since someone has purchased the land, all resources it has be theirs. It's not the case. It could be that you have purchased land, however an individual else is the owner for the wood and trees on the property. Many people don't care whether someone cut the trees surrounding their house so long as their home is safe. What they may not realize is that the trees surrounding can aid in preventing flooding and can be a major threat to the structure. Therefore, it's better to gather all details regarding any timber contracts that are currently in force that are on your land.

I've previously talked about the possibility to drill a hole, installing an septic tank, or installing solar panels in the event that you're not connected with the city's lines for water, sewage, or electricity or electricity. However, it is crucial to ensure that you're in compliance with the regulations set by local authorities when performing this. Concerning the environment and water it is equally important to look around for signs of pollution as well as industrial waste which could create danger to your health in the near future.

In the end, you'll want to ensure that you are covered by title insurance and escrow to ensure that your money are protected in the event that the deal fails due to any reason. They will protect you from any details about the property that the seller may have kept secret.

Although all of these factors are of significance when it comes to purchasing the land needed to construct even normal homes, they are likely to take on greater importance for shipping containers homes due to due to the lack of understanding of the procedure for shipping container homes.

Permits & Regulations

Housing regulations are most likely the most difficult hurdle you might have to conquer in the area you live in. Unfortunately, there isn't a way to get around these rules. The best thing to do is find as much information as you can about the legal requirements your construction must comply with. If it's on the internet or contact with those (if there are any) living in the area that have container homes It's all about obtaining the most information you can. Despite the wide range of variation in the rules across regions There are two distinct things that you should be aware of for construction regulations and permit.

The building codes comprise nothing more than rules for how buildings can be constructed and not. These are the rules that are set in order to ensure the security and safety of those living in the home. This could be related with the types of materials which can be used in the foundation, or even the structural aspects that have to be considered. Certain states allow container homes only in certain sizes, while some require that you possess certain types of designs.

The codes typically originate from The International Code Council (ICC) and are later implemented by local authorities. Although some states, like Mississippi have regulations for the entire state while others have codes that are unique for each city. These codes differ mostly because they depend on local conditions such as humidity and regulations for zoning that streamline urban development.

When it comes to the building regulations for homes built in shipping containers, there are certain things that will be more regulated than others. First, authorities may be looking to ensure uniformity in the appearance of houses in the area. This means that if your layout of your home is unique to the location, there's the possibility that it won't be allowed. Also, there's the matter of site offsets , which is mostly related to how far the building is from the boundaries of your property, as and the distance between adjacent properties. Local authorities are likely to be concerned about the security of your container house and also the plumbing and electrical plans.

I know what you're thinking: that this sounds a bit complex; in fact, sometimes it's. If you follow the procedure below, it might be much easier for you to complete the process. This is a basic outline of how to organize your steps towards obtaining permits:

The plan for your project The reason we talked about this before is that it is difficult to know the details about shipping containers to the vast majority of the population. This is likely to include the authorities who will approve your plans. Therefore, it is crucial to prepare a well-constructed plan before you apply for an permit. Understanding the most important details in detail will aid your case enormously. This includes the plan, the electrical plans and plumbing plans and the timeline that could be set of the work. It is possible to create an organized plan that includes all of these details and then use it in your pitch to authorities.

Research: In addition to the laws and codes for building in your locality It is also important to look into the regulations for your local Homeowner's Association (HOA) just to be sure you are on the right side.

Develop a rapport with local authorities. The more time you spend with officials at the local level and respond to their questions and concerns, the better for your business. Be sure to answer their questions in a clear manner, however, remember that providing them information isn't only the most important deal to do here. The more you can establish rapport with them the more forthcoming they'll be with regards to the different types of permits you might need. Often, separate permits are needed for electrical systems, heating plumbing, and so on. This will help you avoid a lot of problems.

Submissions and forms It is necessary to complete an application form with the local authorities to pay the cost of. You might also have to provide the plans mentioned previously, photos as well as structural engineering calculations and more, depending the location you're in.

On-site inspections: Locally-run authorities usually determine the amount of building inspections that are required prior to the time. It is generally an ideal idea to bring your contractor along during these inspections as it is he is the one who must incorporate construction codes in the building.

Final approvals: At the time this process is completed you'll have various documents that allow your project to go ahead. This will usually include documents like the Certificate of Zoning Compliance, Certificate of Completion and Utility Certificate as well as a Certificate Of Occupancy.

Make sure you have all permits needed prior to beginning construction, as non-compliance could result in fines at the very least and even demolitions at worst.

Resolving the Issues of Residents of the Local Area

If you believed that after dealing with the authorities your job was over it's not correct. While obtaining the right permits is likely to be the most crucial step but you also may need to meet with the people you'll be sharing your community with. It might not be that important what their opinions are about the home you've built in your shipping container, but it's because, in the end, it's their home that you live with.

Keep in mind that however indirect it is it may be, they are still an important stakeholder in this. Consider it. What would you think to see your neighbor buy a dirty, rusty vehicle and put in the driveway of your neighbor in which it was constantly running out of oil constantly? Well, I think you're thinking. It's not a rusty old automobile. It's a shipping containers home in which you're planning to reside! Yes, that's what happens when you're unfamiliar or human nature. If we don't have a clear understanding of things and things, we tend to think the worst of things and people. This is the way we're designed to defend ourselves from risk.

If your neighbors aren't aware of shipping container houses they may be inclined to believe that the size of the container right next to them could impact their property's worth. This is the reason that you should discuss with them prior to the event and inform them about the plans you have in mind and how it's not going to cause problems for them either whether now or in the future. When they're informed that you aren't planning to transport a piece of garbage into their area and they're likely to be enthralled and may even be favorable to your container's return journey.

It's time to start the building process. We are just only a few steps away from having access to the container.

Financing Your Shipping Container Home

As previously mentioned, people choose shipping container homes due to their affordable price. Many would rather dip into their savings to build their homes from scratch every homeowner has the option of building their own homes. In such cases the mortgage may be the best option for these people.

The most important thing is not to get caught up by the word has become a dreadful word that we fear so much. Be aware that the loan amount for a conventional house will be much higher. It is, of course dependent on the style you envision. It is possible to spend many thousands of expenses when choosing the container house. However, if this is the case, the reason for choosing an apartment in a shipping container will likely be to build a stunning, elegant design , not to create an affordable house. However, as we'll see throughout this guide In most cases it is entirely likely to be able to create a compromise with comfort, affordability and design all wrapped into one gorgeous home.

The issue is that institutions aren't prepared to provide these loans. The inexperience with shipping container homes, which we discussed earlier, is a problem also. Although loans are available to RVs, shipping containers aren't yet mainstream enough to allow this process to be straightforward. I think it's only a issue of time before banks and lenders recognize the enormous potential of the market and get onto the bandwagon.

The situation is a bit tense. It's particularly difficult to obtain financing for container homes due to the nature of what is considered an "property" to these lending institutions. The majority of lenders don't consider a structure to be a real estate property until it is permanently connected with the foundation.

However, even if you do have the funds you do, there are many hurdles you'll have to get over. For instance, lenders may have specific guidelines on the conditions they'll give you money. Some lenders may not provide the cash until the house is completed, while some may prefer to wait until they have the approvals and certificates from local authorities. The issue of collateral is also a concern for these lenders when it comes to the purchase with shipping container houses. Be aware that they are taking a risk when they offer you money, and they must consider the most likely scenario in which you're an insolvent. A shipping container doesn't have any value until it is transformed into the home you're looking to purchase.

With that said there isn't anything bad. There are companies that can meet the needs of financing your container home. If you do a quick Google search will reveal names such as Acorn Financing and Container Home Financing that claim to know the specifics of container homes and try to tweak traditional loans to meet the demands of the new generation of homeowners. Numerous lenders have appeared over the past few years such as Rocket Mortgage, Sofi, Lendingtree, Beeline, and Better. It is possible to start looking to see their rates, examine them and choose the one that fits you the most. Remember that obtaining the pre-approval that clearly states the loan is intended for shipping containers can go a long way, and will allow you to stick to the schedule.

Chapter 4: Doing the Foundation (Literally)

It doesn't take any kind of rocket scientist to understand that the foundation you construct your home on is an essential aspect of the home's design. Geologicallyspeaking, the earth is moving at a speed that we don't even be aware of. Yet, even though these movements are not noticeable the level of your home can dramatically be affected over the course of time. This is the crucial aspect that makes foundations a top place in building codes. Therefore, it is sensible to spend plenty of time attempting to comprehend the intricate details of selecting and laying the foundation.

Be aware that even though you can complete this process and purchase of the container in the same transaction but you need to prepare your foundation before your container is delivered to the location. Therefore, it is by conducting your research before you go. There are several kinds of foundations you'll have to think about when choosing one that is best suited to your budget and the requirements of the structure of your home.

Types of Foundation

The most frequent mistake homeowners make when they build their homes in shipping containers is choosing one of the incorrect bases. This can ruin the dream of owning and building the home of a shipping container. The kind of foundation you pick is contingent upon a number of variables. There could be some fundamental and secondary considerations you should look at. The primary considerations are typically the requirements for structural structure and budget, while secondary considerations could include the soil type (soft or hard) and the quantity of containers you intend to build with.

The two major types of foundation are referred to as shallow and deep foundations. For example, soft soil could require stronger and deeper foundations, perhaps even as deep as ten meters and hard soil might be able to do without foundations.

Particularly, foundations are of four kinds:

Concrete pier

Slab on grade

Pile

Strip

Let's examine each of these in more detail.

Concrete Piers Foundation

This kind of foundation is one that is easy to construct for all of you DIY-ers. It's cost-effective and suitable for all types of homes built from shipping containers. They don't require any special equipment that is difficult to locate for someone who does it on their own.

The foundation is comprised of concrete blocks, usually with the dimensions 50cm fifty centimeters x 50 centimeters x 50 cm. They are reinforced by steel wires that increase their strength, and assists in securing huge loads. The most common method is to put one block on each of the corners, and then put another one in the middle, just to ensure safety. They do not require any excavation at all. Another benefit is that they hold containers at a level above the ground. This ensures that there will not be condensation on the surface of the container because of plenty of air circulation.

Slab On Grade Foundation

Slab on grade is completely different approaches to foundation. It is a homogeneous slab of cement that is created by digging out the ground. It is used primarily when the soil is very soft and is costly contrasted to pier foundations due to the equipment needed.

Imagine digging a trench in the ground larger than the area of the home you are designing and then placing concrete slabs in the area. The slab will usually be smaller than the container. It is a stronger basis than concrete pilings since it is securely anchored in the ground, and the weight of the container is evenly distributed across. Because it doesn't allow any space underneath the structure, it will prevent the possibility of termite invasion. One disadvantage is that once the concrete is set it is not able to connect to gas or water pipelines If you want to drill into the concrete, it will need to be dug into. Additionally, if slabs on grade foundations are utilized in cold conditions there is a possibility of loss of heat via the base of containers.

Pile Foundation

Another foundation type which is useful for those with soft soil is the pile foundation. It is the most costly foundation type and isn't one that DIYers can do. It requires a thorough understanding of the process and large equipment to dig into the foundation.

The idea behind this kind of foundation is, since the soil's top layer is not strong enough to hold the foundation the solid round steel pipes are dug into soil until they strike the hard rock layer. The tubes are solidly anchored to this layer, and the concrete slab is then placed over each one. The result is grid-like tubes of steel that look like concrete piers above the ground. They can be used to provide support for the container home.

Strip Foundation

It is also referred to as trench foundation, and is ideal to shipping container homes that are located with soft soil. It is the middle ground for those split between concrete pier and slab-on-grade foundations. It allows you to lay a concrete strip around the edges of your foundation, instead of making a full blocks of cement. This can drastically reduce the cost.

In moist soils there is a variant of a fully concrete foundations is possible with a thin strip of rubble that is loose is underneath the concrete, so that the water can drain quickly. However, be aware that this type of foundation does not offer the same strength as slab on grade. It isn't able to handle the earthquake's seismicity.

You must make an educated decision on which foundation is the most. There are those who choose foundations that are much more sturdy than that required for their home. It's an option that is better than having foundations that can't allow for the load and can stop your construction midway. It is important to talk with your designer, contractor and structural engineer before deciding which one of these types of foundations to select and be sure that you're following the building codes in force.

The Strength of Concrete

As you might have guessed that a significant portion of the strength of your foundation is dependent on the concrete used to build it. Therefore, it is not unwise to consider concrete's strength separately since it serves as the foundation for your home's container.

The durability of the concrete you make use of is evaluated by various factors.

Compressive strength is a widely measured measure of the strength of concrete. It's the amount of force that concrete is able to withstand without becoming compressed or expanding or shrinking.

Tensile strength refers to the capacity of concrete to withstand cracking and breaking. It is the time it is for concrete to break when exposed to high Tensile strength, which is in essence an inverse pull force.

Flexural strength refers to the degree to which concrete is able to bend. This is usually measured through the loading of a cement block in the middle of concrete.

It's obviously, not required that you are aware of all the different concrete strengths, however it may be helpful to help you understand the significance of the report by a geotechnical engineer. The report may also mention "C15 concrete" in reference to the strength that is generally recognized. However, C30 is extremely strong concrete. The former is constructed by a 1:2:5 ratio of of cement as well as sand and gravel while the latter is an ratio of 1:2:3.

If you require more quantity of cement, it's recommended to get it delivered directly to your construction site ready to use. If you only require smaller amounts you could even make it yourself. One thing you must remember that you must thoroughly mix all of the constituents as otherwise it could cause a decrease in strength, which , in turn, could weaken your structural strength.

One of the primary things to be aware of when working with cement is the process of curing. Only when it's fully curing will it reach the required strength. The process begins when mixing the cement and water. It is vital to keep the temperature of the surrounding area within the range of a specific amount while spraying water over the cement that is curing to ensure it remains wet. The curing procedure and will differ for different brands and it is recommended to check the label for the specific steps to follow.

Laying the concrete in a variety of Weather Conditions

The concrete is just a small part of the construction of the foundation, but it could by itself be quite an intricate process. It is essential to be aware of the whole process since doing it correctly is crucial to the security of the entire construction.

Calculating the amount of concrete needed could be determined by multiplying required width by the length x the thickness of slab. Once you have this information, it's time to place an order for the cement and start work. The process of laying the concrete is divided into various steps that are carried out over several days.

Preparation The process of getting the ground prepared by clearing any obstacles that could hinder the cement's installation. This involves excavation and leveling the ground by removing rocks, grass and other vegetation. It is also possible to compress the ground by pounding it.

Forming The steel mesh and the shape you select enters the picture. If it's a slab you'll need to create frames that give the exact dimensions you'll be required to pour the cement over.

Pouring: This is typically accomplished using a pump, which aids in pouring concrete to the right areas. It will need to be smoothed out as it is being poured to provide an even surface.

Finish The upper surface of the top is smoothed by trowels to create a smooth top.

Curing: The surface is allowed to rest and build up from within. The process is thought to last around 28 days, though it is the initial week that's believed to be the most crucial. Curing agents can be used to improve the durability even more.

The whole process is susceptible to climate changes for obvious reasons. Since the concrete must remain moist in order to be cured, it is vital to protect it by direct sun. It is possible to put up shades to shield the concrete from the intense sunlight. One suggestion is to make use of cold water when mixing the cement and to spray the ground prior to placing the concrete. This helps to hold the moisture in and helps in the curing process. It is also advantageous to place the concrete during cooler times in the day, perhaps early in the morning or shortly at sunset to keep from extreme temperatures.

In the same way, pouring concrete at temperatures below zero can be a challenge. It is essential to ensure that the place you intend to lay the concrete is clean and is free of any remaining snow, ice, or perhaps stagnant or water. The slab should be insulated with blankets the moment you have poured the concrete and for the duration of its cure. Avoid exposure to low temperatures by taking off the blankets immediately. Take it slowly so that cracks aren't created. In the event of rainy days, you should avoid pouring concrete completely. In the absence of taking weather conditions into consideration now could cost you dearly. Therefore, ensure that you be aware of the forecast for weather before you begin to lay the concrete.

Attaching the Container

If you don't properly secure the container onto the base, the rest your efforts are in vain. It is crucial to take as much care in fixing the container to the foundation as you do in building the foundation.

Whatever foundation you decide to use the container is generally secured with the help of the steel plate. It should be at minimum a quarter-inch thick. The more thick it is, the more durable it is deemed to be. The steel plate is placed over concrete. The ideal time for this is before the concrete is set. The steel plate is composed of steel rods that are perpendicular to its underside that will sink into the cement to ensure that the plate is steady and in a level position. Be sure to follow your local building regulations here, as different local authorities might require the process to be carried out differently. The container is then placed on the plate.

Although the above method is ideal for stability however, there are other methods to attach the container. For instance, you can use J hooks to secure the container to the rebar within the concrete or bolting it to the concrete using anchors. This method is less complicated than other methods to attach the foundation, but in reality, it's not as sturdy.

In many areas there may not an obligation that you have to fix containers to foundations. You could simply put it on top and then be finished with it. However, be aware of any instability. This is generally recommended when you plan for the possibility of moving your container at some point in the future since welded plates create a more challenging task. Keep in mind that the way you secure the container onto your foundation can affect the likelihood of the ability to obtain financing or coverage for the home you own, like we have discussed in the previous section.

Chapter 5: Buying the Container

The most exciting part of the trip is now here, when you can actually buy the home that you'll live in. It's a thrilling purchase. Because this is a decision which you make on your own, without guidance from the engineer, contractor or architect, this could be quite thrilling. It is a decision you take purely on the way you envision your living space to look. You can decide what size, whether small and "tiny" (as it's commonly described) you would like your home to look like.

I've spoken to numerous homeowners of shipping containers who wish they had the information they have now on the study that goes into the whole process. Many people don't know about high-cube containers, or the other options covered in this book before they start to build their homes. When they learn that they don't, it's usually too late, and all they can do is look back and wish they'd taken a different approach.

That's why it's essential to review your needs and make an effort to match them to the top options available in the market. The goal of making your home as beautiful as you can is essential since both you and your loved ones members deserve to have a place in which you are able to release all tension and not accumulate. You may not be aware of that at first however, living in a small space is a lot more challenging in the event that regrets also fill up space. A thorough investigation will be your only chance to stay clear of this.

Where can I buy?

After you've completed all of your research, you're ready to purchase the home. One of the things that confuses buyers at this point is finding a trustworthy dealer in the field of shipping container homes. Today, buying online is the best choice. This is particularly true for new containers. If you want to purchase a brand new container, conduct an Google search and lots of relevant search results will appear. The best method to do this is to get quotes from a variety of businesses and then choose the most appropriate choice in terms of cost and the location. There is no need to worry about the state of the container as it is

fresh and arrive directly to your place
from the site of its birth. factory.

The used containers are more difficult
to find. It is also possible to purchase
done online, however it's a risky option
since you don't get to inspect the
condition of the container before it will
arrive at your home. Do not do this. I've
seen too many customers who believed
in the word of the business on the
quality, only to end up with damaged,
beaten-up containers. Because of the
magnitude of these the containers,
returning them could be a different
matter altogether.

Alibaba, eBay, Green Cube Network
Alibaba, eBay, Green Cube Network
Gumtree are just a few of the websites
where you can get containers
from. While they offer the convenience
of shopping from your home, you won't
be able to make any other choices but
to look up reviews on the
internet. Although this is a good option
for the majority all other items, for
something as big that a large shipping
box it might not be worth the
cost. Another thing be very aware of is
where the item is shipped from. If it's
not a container that is local, that means

you'll be liable for massive shipping costs that could drain the savings you had been hoping to achieve when you made the decision to purchase an apartment in a shipping container in place of traditional dwelling. This is the reason the containers are sitting in the port in the first place. There is no anyone to claim them, do you remember?

If you purchase directly from the business isn't a good choice, as they might not want to offer just two or three containers. Be aware that these companies sell in bulk and dealers are able to get better prices because of the quantity they purchase. It is possible to contact these firms to find out whether they have any local distributors and dealers in your local area. If you are in an area with a port your best option for you is to visit the port by yourself, look for the container depot, where the companies that lease or sell containers are able to store empty containers and purchase from a firm directly. Because many of them would like to eliminate the containers accumulating and taking the space of their premises, you may be able to negotiate an advantageous deal as well.

The best compromise in between an older container and a brand-new container could be one-trip containers. These are containers that have been on the move for between 75 and 90 days and are not more than one year old. They're typically in better condition than older containers. They're not much more costly than an older container, and compensate for the cost increase by being more secure and simpler to frame as well as the insulation procedure.

No matter what container you choose to purchase If you're buying off the internet, ensure that you examine the container on your own. Remember the advice we gave before that "newer" doesn't necessarily mean better. A single-trip container could be badly damaged even in one transport.

Physical Inspection is a must

I recommend that everyone have all their questions answered when choosing the shipping containers they want to use. If you are purchasing a brand-new container, obviously, there isn't much to choose other than dimensions and colors. If, however, you're looking to purchase a used container the physical inspection is essential. In the ideal scenario, there must be a pre-purchase inspection and an after-purchase inspection since the implications of each could differ.

The containers used for shipping and the manufacturing facilities that make them are subject to strict inspection rules when they are being used to transport essential items. This is to make sure that they're structurally sound as they travel overseas. There are various standards these inspections have to meet for shipping , however, to be able to ship containers, these inspections do not have to be as rigorous. It is possible to examine the container and decide the appropriateness of the container to your needs or not.

However it is the "looking" component of the inspection must be able to spot problems quickly. It is suggested that you take as many photographs as you can of the container's inside, so that you can review them even more later. It is likely to be dark interior. Although light might come in from one direction however, it might not be enough to see the small issues. Therefore, make sure to walk inside with an emergency flashlight. Additionally, a useful item is a step stool to ensure you are able to thoroughly examine the ceiling and the top part wall. A hammer could be useful, also, as it will ensure that there isn't any rust that is threatening the foundation inside the storage container.

Here are a few items to be looking for in an inspection:

More information are available on CSC Plate

This is among the first things to look into the container. It is important to know that the Container Safety Convention is one of the safety standards containers must adhere to. It is the CSC plate, which is referred to by the Combined Data Plate, gives you all the data you should know regarding the containers. It's a metallic plate that's which is attached to the container that contains the required information. It'll provide you with several information, including your Container Identification Number. This is among the most pertinent details for you. The number may look like this: ATHU51236-9. The initial three letters indicate the owner's code, while the fourth letter is the group code of the product The following six digits represent the container's serial number, and the final number is called the check digit, which guarantees that the container was registered in a correct manner. If you are inspecting the container, ensure that you confirm that the exact container is delivered to you. The identification number can help confirm this.

Other information is also provided on the plate, such as the ACEP/PES number, type code along with Classification Society approval, which guarantees the solidity of the container. However, it might not be of any use for you as a homeowner.

Rusty Metal

This is among the most crucial factors that demands your focus. It will ultimately determine how durable and sturdy your home will be. The surface rust may not pose a issue. The structural rust, on other hand, is an indication of danger. It is so widespread that it could cause gaping holes in the steel. Even if the holes can be patched the chances are that they'll appear in other areas within the construction. In the event that the container's at a stage that is too damaged to be fixed, then it's best to find an alternative container.

The fascinating thing about this is that it doesn't require advanced technology to know whether the corrosion is structural or just surface-level. Simply tap the surface that is rusted using the (hammer). When you can hear distinctively different sound after doing this opposed to tapping the non-rusted part, then the rust may be structural and you should keep away from it. Another method to determine this is to block any light sources that stream into the container and see if one ray of light penetrates the container. If you shut the door of the container, it should be like nighttime in the container. If you can see the smallest hint of light, it's a sign that walls are falling off due to corrosion.

You should inspect for rust on the wall of your storage container for rust. There are times where rust is only limited to the spaces that you need to cut in order to install window and doors. This is a good thing since you can get an excellent container at cheap cost. Make sure you have your plans clear when checking the container because even a tiny error could lead to you get an unsound container.

Another area that is important to examine is the bottom of the container's bottom. Most people do not pay attention to this since while it's important but it is difficult to check this area after the container has been placed on the surface. The ideal time to inspect the bottom of containers is when it's being removed from the truck and thus hanging in air. If you're planning to build a new roofing system for your home the container's roof is no longer relevant, and it doesn't matter if the container is worn out because you're going cut it anyway.Be sure to examine the locks and doors on the containers.

But what is more important, though is the frame of the container's frame. The container usually has 12 steel beams which form the edges of their sides. It is vital that these are in good condition. Keep in mind that whenever you cut any area of the container, you'll reduce its structural strength. If the beams are in good working order they will be much simpler to strengthen the structure.

Finally, I strongly suggest that you remove the floors of your container completely since these floors have been treated by pesticides. Even if the floors appear to be in good condition, it isn't a problem since for the moment it could appear like you're saving cash, but you should be certain that it's going to ruin the health of your family and friends ones health.

Shipping Container Grades

While the history of the container's owner is available on it's CSC plaque, one can't know for certain the location it's been in or what it was employed for. The only thing you be certain about a container's age is whether the container's brand new or used. It is possible to choose shipping container grade to make your choice. Although it is true that homes in shipping containers are graded on the basis of their condition, it's important to keep in mind that there isn't an any industry-wide standard that applies to these classes. The result is that, while one business may give a container the "A" grade however, it is not guaranteed that another business will award an identical grade. Be aware that the grade is subjective. What matters to you isn't as much the grade , but the circumstances that caused the grade. It is crucial to seek out the criteria of the company that they use to grade the container, and then make a decision based on the information you have gathered.

To talk about the new and old classifications more, the new containers could be classified into brand-new containers or one-trip container and renovated containers. We've seen what the brand new containers and one-trip ones are. The problem is that refurbishment of containers isn't as simple to comprehend because of the ambiguity of the terminology. It isn't possible to say for sure what qualifies as a "renovated" container. It may be better to label them recycled containers that have had some minor repairs. The amount of the repairs is what you'll need to decide by yourself during the inspection.

Prior to that, classifications were the categories of water-tight, wind-tight, and cargo-worthy and containers that are water-tight. Containers that are cargo-worthy are those which may be damaged and worn out, but they still serve their purpose of transporting goods in accordance with the Container Safety Convention (CSC) standards. If you're looking for used containers, then cargo-worthy is the best option.

Containers that are water-tight or wind-proof are the ones not being used for transport nowadays. They may appear a little less attractive than cargo-worthy ones, however, the distinctions could be insignificant enough to not make a difference. For instance, the distinction between a container's being described as cargo-worthy and wind - and water-tight may be as thin as the extent of a dent within the former that is greater than the inspection standards permit. Keep in mind that minor dents may be filled in easily, but the larger the dent are, they're more challenging it is to ensure that the container is adequately insulated. Experts typically look for damage using a straight-cut wood beam. It might seem like an insignificant thing, but this is the reason your judgement is vital. The container may be marked waterproof and windproof, but it could be able to be an excellent price for the price.

Containers that are in an unsatisfactory state to be referred to as wind and water-tight are referred to "as are." They're getting dented and rusty, and may not be appropriate to be used in construction at all. If you are considering purchasing one, it is unattainable for you, buying after an check is questionable since there is no warranty on the containers. If you are in doubt about them, avoid them completely.

Based on this list, while brand new containers are great for your home for shipping containers old ones can provide what you require. The answer is dependent on the decision you make as you examine it physically and pay attention to the small and big things, and then taking into your home's design position, design and more.

Once you've passed the physical test then you're now prepared to buy the container. However, remember that it's only a container. If you want it to feel as home, you'll need to ensure that the insides reflect the person you are.

Chapter 6: The Interiors: Putting them in Place

The Interiors of the Container Home

And there it is! A shipping container set in the ground! It's time to transform the dingy, metallic interior into a warm and livable space. When your container is delivered, you will have received approval from the local authorities. At least that's what it is supposed to be. It is now time to implement your plans with care. Installing the interiors is quite a complicated task. If you're doing this yourself, prepare yourself for a lot of cutting, measuring, and additional blueprints and plans.

There are a lot of samples of plans on the internet. However, the problem with these is that they're rarely accurate. Selecting a random home plan is not helpful to anyone. This is a crucial step which will determine how comfortable you will feel in your house for the long term. Therefore, make sure that you make it the right way. While it's fine drawing inspiration for your design from these templates, it's recommended to engage an engineer and architect in your area to implement your concepts in a more custom effective, practical and cost-effective manner.

If you choose to do it on yourself, then it may be better for you to get your designs downloaded from trusted online sources instead of looking to cut costs by going to the wrong areas. Another good option if want to cut costs on hiring experts to design your residence for you, is to contact students studying architecture and engineering and also upcoming architects in your local area. Although larger firms may charge for their own brand however, the junior architects could provide you with the perfect design for less. In the end, they have the basic knowledge you require, and working with you could be just the experience they're looking for.

Floor Plans

Interiors of shipping containers could make some people think of being simple and basic because of the small space that has to be designed. What they aren't aware of is that smaller spaces require greater planning and organization than bigger ones. This is where floor plans are crucial. Understanding the size of the area you're planning to build is vital. The hiring of professionals for this task is recommended , not just to ensure precision in calculations for the living space , but in addition to ensure that the layouts work effectively. For example, a design that puts the kitchen and bathroom in opposite corners of the container could not be the best choice for more efficient and less expensive plumbing.

The various websites that offer sample plans online offer an array of choices. Before you decide on all of them you must decide on the most important factors. What size of space do you require? What is your experience living in smaller areas? It may be beneficial to have an existing container house prior to creating your own home to gain an understanding of the space considerations within a limited space. It may not be a viable alternative for everyone, however Airbnb offers shipping container rentals in several areas. The living space in these homes could be very informative as to what you could incorporate into the floor plan of your home.

As you might think, the designs and choices vary widely in the 20 and 40 feet. The variety of choices for using different containers can be confusing. It is important to analyze every option thoroughly and carefully to avoid confusion due to analysis. Many find this stage as the most difficult due to the fact that they are trying to do everything at once , and this could be a significant obstacle in the construction of your own container home. Remember, the concept is not to try to fit everything in, but instead focus on the items you value most for you within your smaller space.

Even if you decide to keep your plans off of the web, there's something you can create to make smaller living spaces appear larger. Let's look at some of these suggestions.

Doors: You might not notice that it occupies a larger area the doors of conventional design can take up quite a bit of space. Take a look at the swept space that the doors have. It is not a place to use for any other purpose unless you would like it to get into to hinder opening of the door. This can be extremely restrictive for a home with a shipping container. A great solution is to install sliding doors. They do not require any extra space since their swept area is just zero. As their name implies they smoothly slide along the straight line. Two kinds that slide doors include pocket doors as well as barn doors. Barn doors are suspended by an overhead track that keeps doors in position pocket doors come with a more practical design that can be retracted into a pocket of kind in the wall.

Furniture: Another aspect you must think about when you're trying to maximize the space of your home's containers is the amount of space taken up by furniture. This does not mean the area that furniture occupies but rather the space it doesn't use. One method of furnishing effectively is to buy furniture that is built to ensure that you don't waste space. A lot of container owners opt for this option, but keep in mind that custom-made furniture will significantly increase the cost of your home.

If you're looking to cut out the cost, a better option is to make use of convertible furniture. By choosing the best type of daybeds and convertible couches will provide your home with the perfect appearance while making sure that you do not compromise on space or utility.

Wall-mounts: Wall mounts can be great for saving space. Wall-mounted televisions and wall-mounted desks are popular among homeowners who live in containers. They can create perfect spaces for entertainment and workstations without sacrificing space. Although many aspects of these are commonplace, like wall-mounted TVs and desks, for instance may not be initially what springs to thoughts. Desks that fold, even when you're not using they can fold to be tucked back to the wall.

Larger rooms with open spaces: In areas, you might not be aware of how much of your living space is covered by walls that surround your home. In contrast smaller spaces can allow you to appreciate this fact far more. Making use of other methods to partition rooms will greatly improve the space you have and give your home the appearance of a "new-age" style. This could range from folding panels and curtains dividers to double-sided fireplaces or shelves for books. Kitchens that are open are a excellent way to give your home a contemporary appearance while preserving space.

The lighting and color scheme Living in a tiny area like the one of homes built in shipping containers will show you that it'sn't just about the space available but also the mental state of the individual living in it. Be aware that dull and dingy spaces seem to encroach on your more than vibrant and lively ones. Many homeowners opt to put in high-quality windows at their residences for this reason. The light and view can make people feel less of a space restriction. In addition with regards to lights, the traditional way of lighting demands large equipment such as an sconce for the wall or a lamp. LED lighting, on other hand, are great when you're looking to reduce the long-term cost of electricity and can also be a valuable desk, floor as well as wall spaces. The use of a vibrant design that speaks to your personality and style is a simple, low-cost method of making even small spaces appear lively.

Plenty of Light and the Best View

Mirrors: Mirrors might not actually increase the size of the room that you live in however they can be very beneficial in making you feel as if you are in it. They aren't for everyone but when they're integrated into the right way with careful idea, they can improve your space in a fashionable and affordable way.

It may appear like common sense, however they can be extremely beneficial to your floor plan when used correctly. It is strongly recommended that you consider these choices when designing your floor plans instead of performing haphazard modifications once you're half way through.

A Few Great Designs Across the Globe

As the popularity of shipping containers for homes grows, stunning and fascinating designs are appearing across the globe. The designs, as well as aiding in the awareness of the possibility of living in a shipping container and boosting the aesthetic quotient up a notch higher. In this article, we'll examine some of the best designs, and then we will look at a few house plans to inspire you.

PV14 house: This amazing structure is situated inside Dallas, Texas, and was featured in the film PV14 Home: Luxury shipping container home located in Dallas, Texas on the YouTube channel Shelter Mode (Shelter Mode, 2018b). The house is constructed using 14 shipping containers to create the form of a single-storey residence, spread across about 3700 square. feet. in living area. The home is comprised of a living room on the first floor, a massive living area on the first floor and a penthouse that has access to a stunning balcony on the upper floor. The property is built with the appearance of a tall tower of shipping containers at the center which give it an ultra-modern style. The house is finished with the longest swimming pool which is a perfect reflection of the towering container. Whoever believed that shipping containers are just for minimalists certainly hasn't seen this home.

Taynr The company's tagline that reads "You do not have to get huge to make it home," Taynr provides a variety of single container prefabricated homes with contemporary and modern designs. The model featured in their video "TAYNR 2/1" Model Shipping Container Home on their YouTube channel features an elegant design that is simple and elegant with just the right amount of. The house is perfect for couples. This home has everything you need: a living room, kitchen, toilet, and a bathroom, bedroom, and a gorgeous deck outside. What more could one ask for?

The Manifesto House located within Curacavi, Chile, this unique container house was developed for James And Mau Arquitectura as well as Infiniski. It is distinctive due to the way that it combines modular design and recycled materials. The living area of the home is 1750 square. feet. by stacking one container over another. We are all aware of Shelter Mode which brings us yet another video called Manifesto House The Container House from James & Mau Arquitectura. Infiniski in Curacavi, Chile. The voiceover here states that almost 90% of the material that is used in this video is recycled, including the container and the insulation made from recycled paper or cellulite as it's commonly called.

Casa Incubo This modern design was showcased on YouTube channel Salvador Solis Rizo in the video Casa Incubo | Shipping Container Home | Container Architecture. In Costa Rica, this home is built using eight 40 foot high cubes. A significant amount of weight has been devoted to natural light through the use of glass walls as well as cross-air ventilation. The living room centrally located is a huge space , which is accentuated more by the abundance of light and the light shades utilized in the interiors. The other areas of the home seem to blend perfectly into the central area. This area doubles as a workspace, too. the first floor is comprised of the dining room, kitchen as well as a office and photo gallery. The second floor houses bedrooms, while the third floor houses an open-air terrace that has the most beautiful roof garden.

The Crossbox It is a stunning piece of art made in France. A glance at this modern and innovative style is enough to entice you. It is made of four 20 footers It provides a decent 1,120 square. feet. for living spaces. This home is perfect for families and includes an open-plan living area with a kitchen and dining area, as well as an bathroom on the first floor. It also has three bedrooms as well as bathrooms on the first floor. On YouTube, the channel Home Interior Plus gives you an insight into few photos of this house in their video, Cargo Container Homes eco-friendly Crossbox House designed by CG Architectes.

Grillagh Water House: This container home will take you to a magical landscape. A stark contrast between modern design against the rustic rural scenes is nothing less than stunning. Channel 4 Lifestyle video on YouTube named Kevin McCloud Reminisces About His Favorite home, a shipping container Kevin's Grandest Design showcases the beauty and also gives viewers a brief glimpse of the purchasing and building process.

It is possible to go on since there are many other distinctive living spaces created from these boxes. I encourage you to take a the time to look at the most of them feasible when you are thinking of your own ideas. However, it is equally important to recognize that home designs and design are two different things. Making sure you have the proper dimensions is vital in this process. Let's take a look at some websites that can assist you download home plans for free. plans.

Etsy: Etsy is a worldwide online marketplace that focuses on handmade products. This is an excellent spot to get samples of plans to purchase directly from the designers. The cost of these plans differ widely. Make sure you are focusing on the design and not the price.

Pinup Houses The site offers access to a variety of paid plans that are specifically tailored to your requirements. They are specifically designed especially for DIY builders. They aren't in a shipping container section and it could be exhausting to browse through their many designs to choose a home style that is right for your needs.

Modern Dwellings The exact name implies, this business provides minimalist and ultra-modern living spaces. In addition, the company offers prefabricated studios that can be built in containers and the Model One plan if you want to build your own. However, they have only one design for studios which is called that of the True Studio, which means anyone seeking an affordable family home may not get much value from this.

Australian Design Services: This is an Australian business that offers hundreds of home plans you can buy. The site is user-friendly, and allows you to easily search for designs for homes built using shipping containers as well as other home design services they provide.

Although these are all excellent sources, be aware there is a web brimming with many more of these websites as well as YouTube channel. All you need to do is click just a few clicks and an abundance of knowledge about the shipping container will be available to you. It is important to avoid getting overwhelmed by all of them. Making your own home isn't something you'll do every day and is worthy of all your focus, effort and effort. Make sure to conduct your research prior to getting into action.

Floor Selections

Another crucial aspect to consider to consider is what flooring material you choose to use. Flooring is essential for temperature control which is a significant problem for shipping container homes. It is therefore important to consider it as thoroughly as you can.

As we have discussed, many shipping containers have bamboo or plywood floorings, which I strongly suggest getting rid of. Another alternative is to use these floors and then cover them with epoxy. It is a compound which provides a slip-resistant surface to the flooring. This makes sure that harmful chemicals present in the flooring are held underneath the coating, thus greatly diminishing the risk of toxins infiltrating your body. The coating also helps to make the flooring more sturdy.

There are many other options to think about. If the look of wood is something you are drawn to it is possible to opt for faux wooden vinyl plansks. These will give a striking rustic appeal to your house since they are available in a variety of hues of timber. They are usually preferred in their living and offices. One of the best options for bathroom flooring is called coin vinyl. It's water-resistant and keeps the floor from becoming slippery.

If you are planning to install carpets as flooring ensure that they are not too dense as they can trap heat which makes the containers hotter during the summer months. Carpets are an excellent choice when it comes to multi-storey container homes since they assist in soundproofing. Another benefit suitable for shipping container houses with small space is that carpets are able to aid in the internal separation of the living space without the requirement for partitions that create additional space.

Electric & Plumbing Plans

The next step in the process of interiors is the installation of the electrical and plumbing system. This isn't something you can take lightly since it will affect your daily routine like nothing other.

Plumbing can be accomplished by using copper pipes or PEX. If you're not familiar with soldering PEX could be an ideal alternative. When installing plumbing, remember that you'll have to cut into your flooring and attach it to the line of water beneath your home. If you are laying concrete, you'll need to create an opening that the plumbing is connected to main lines. The holes you drill will be in the floor to create these spaces. When you do this, it is important to pay attention to the area you're drilling holes. It is not advisable to drill holes directly through the structural beams that are the main reason for the structural stability of your container.

I frequently hear that, since these houses have smaller spaces, it can't be a toilet within the home and you must build an outside structure. It isn't true. If you have the right plan then you will not be able to just put the toilet in, but also place it in a way that reduces the plumbing costs.

If you are in need of the electrical aspect, I would strongly suggest hiring an electrician since this job could be dangerous. Make sure to be done in accordance with local building regulations as well as the National Electrical Standards. When installing electrical wires in metallic containers, it's crucial to be aware that the consequences of wiring that is not properly installed not just electrocution that is fatal, but also the risk of the fire resulting from overheating.

Building a Home from the Plans

If you have all of the above and you're technically prepared for the insulation stage, which we'll go over in the following chapter. However, this is only true for those who plan only a single container house. If you're planning to build an even larger home using multiple containers, it will be useful in order to record specific aspects.

In the first place, as previously mentioned when you have a number of containers at home, it's usually recommended to buy containers made by the same maker because there are slight differences which can cause the aligning of the containers challenging. The joining of the containers is something that you can make yourself. There are kits for container joining available in the marketplace as well.

Absolutely Stacked Shipping Containers

Containers for shipping, which we've often observed, are comparable to Lego blocks placed on top of one another. According to some sources, these containers could be stacked up at a maximum height of 10 containers without extra reinforcement. However, remember that this is just for shipping containers designed to transport cargo. When you begin cutting into the sides to create windows and doors, those numbers aren't true in any way. As long as they're not reinforced significantly, they may not be able to withstand the entire load.

The key to stacking containers over one another is that the design needs to be in a manner that ensures an even distribution of the load. While looking at a pile of containerized shipping units, it might seem like one is sitting on the top of the firstone, it's not the case in any way. It's the beams that support the structure rather than the roofing which allow for a proper distribution of containers' weight. Therefore, if the smaller container were to be placed on top of a larger container, the entire structure could collapse as the beams no longer supporting the weight that is placed on the top.

The stacking of the containers one on one another is likely the most cost-effective method of building an multi-container house. We have seen too many containers that do not necessarily adhere to the guidelines above and are able to look gorgeous while remaining completely secure. This is due to the enthralling power of reinforcement. The more unique the style you choose to follow, the greater structural reinforcement you'll need to build your home with. If you're willing to pay for more for your home, the possibilities of playing with your design are unlimited. All you have to do is ensure that your design meets the guidelines of city's building code. The chance of getting an unusual, edgy design approved into the middle an established neighborhood could be quite low.

Another option to build a house from multiple containers is to set them side-by side. The issue with this strategy is the fact that every container feature the bulging ISO corner fittings, which leave a gap between two containers. A clay-like material known as Backer Rod is often used to fill the gap in a uniform manner. Another option is to use a welding device to join both containers. It is crucial that the space is filled since these gaps could lead to stagnation of water that could eventually result in rusting of containers.

When you have your plans completed, the next thing to complete is to get your home insulated. home to create the relaxing sanctuary that it was intended to be.

Chapter 7. 7 Benefits of Home Design for Shipping Containers

Affordable

The typical cost for such a home or office is very reasonable. It's less expensive to purchase the container and then turn it into a safe and comfortable residence than purchase a typical home in a city that isn't expensive.

A used container can be bought for $1500USD. That's the price you pay for 305 sq yards of space for floor. If you compare it with the cost of traditional structures, it's decent value.

Container homes made of used containers are less expensive to build than traditional construction methods.

Easy to Build and Use

Shipping Container Homes are easy to construct and operate. All you require is a home and a few shipping containers to begin.

Faster, the Better

Shipping Container Homes are enjoying better living than ever before, and will increase in popularity as time passes. At present living in a shipping container house is considered to be attractive by some, however some people are still stunned at the concept of a container house. A few people are uncertain about whether the homes they are considering meet their requirements and demands for living space considering they can provide such luxurious lifestyles while being far from the bustle of life.

Allow Your Imagination to Run Unhindered

Container homes are an affordable alternative to traditional structures. They are healthy warm, safe, and secure living space. Knowing the way that a home in a shipping container operates will help you decide whether this is the right choice for you.

Find Them Where You Want They're There!

Container homes are a rising trend in a variety of real property markets. They are cost-effective, provide excellent insulation as well as energy efficiency. Additionally that the wall of a container-built home are usually one-eighth of the weight of traditional construction materials, such as the steel and concrete. Container homes that are shipped can be transported in complete assembly to any place around the world via shipping or truck, making containers the ideal choice for those looking to relocate their home to a new place but don't have the time for an extended distance move. The increasing popularity of the homes can be evident by the press, as there is a lack of container homes for moving into HGTV is regarded as to be a "home-flipping" catastrophe which results in the homeowners' problems usually being not enough time or the overflowing boxes for moving.

Environment Friendly

How green could the shipping containers that are vibrant be?

Response: They could be as green as you'd prefer them to.

Consider your home as an eco-pod, in case you're planning to travel in a more sustainable direction. If you put some solar panels on your roof, you can produce energy. If you're near the river or a swift-flowing stream, you can make use of hydro.

A "Green/Living Roof" can be added on roof of the containers to in separating and greatly cut down on cooling and heating costs during summer (in during summer).

Personal Style Personal Style

"Shipping Container Homes are rapidly becoming a trend in the field of architecture. Shipping Container Homes are a great option for homeowners who want to include durability, affordability and environmentally friendly materials. This article will look at the top five benefits of owning a container-based home."

A shipping container could be used as a home since they're built to stand up to the elements. They are strong, durable and waterproof. The material used to create them isn't harmful to humans, meaning you won't need to worry about toxic chemicals getting into your home when you reside in one! They are also very affordable when comparison to other building materials, like concrete or wood blocks, which require skilled workers and higher costs for construction.

Shipping Container Homes are built from sustainable materials. This means that they are able to be recycled and reused. "The containers are constructed of high-density, water-resistant corrugated cardboard and fiberboard. They form the floors, walls ceilings, roofs, and walls. The stackable containers are stacked on top of one another to create a 'house' and all the sides are joined together." Shipping Container Homes are also built with local, inexpensive materials such as fiberglass and steel that makes the containers much cheaper.

Shipping Container Homes are available in a variety of sizes that suit all types of individuals, from tiny one-room houses to huge multi-bedroom structures. There are various designs that you can pick from to create the house you've always wanted.

Shipping Container Homes are, in fact, green. They are made of recycled materials, and they help protect the land from being used to build homes and other structures. They're also simple to build, which means there's no need to waste materials while building the structure. They can be constructed in many complex settings such as on stilts or hillsides which are confined in space

They can also be linked to create a

large house which is perfect for your family's requirements.

Shipping Container Homes are also secure. They are water-tight and fireproof and therefore there is no risk of your home being set on flames. They are also able to stand up to earthquakes and other natural disasters since they are sturdy and have all walls constructed of one type of material. They are able to endure wind gusts as in other weather conditions that could harm traditional homes.

Shipping Container Homes have many other uses aside from being used as a home. They can also be used as storage units or studio, or even as an office. The possibilities are limitless when it comes with Shipping Container Homes.

Chapter 8: The Shipping Container Pros and Pros and

There are numerous advantages to using shipping containers to build your home. Shipping containers are flexible sturdy, long-lasting, and environmentally responsible. In this article we will discuss some of the main reasons why shipping containers are experiencing increasing the popularity of building blocks of contemporary design:

They're a fantastic building material. They can be laid out and moved around, cut and then molded into any kind of building, home or office you can imagine. They can be found at home at the beach or in the woods or in a bustling urban region.

It is easy to add on. It's easy to build a home constructed from shipping containers. Because of the modular nature of their design as well as the standard sizes, houses made out of shipping containers can be expanded or modified by using additional shipping containers.

They can be stacked. It is possible to build an entire two-story house at the cost of a small amount because of the stackability the containers. They can be stackable, or placed side-by-side. It is possible to set them perpendicular. The possibilities are endless.

They can be moved, transported, or moved. Shipping containers are built to carry items across oceans via ships, then to ships to be moved by flatbed trucks to land. Because of their size and design they can be built and later transported to a construction site or transferred from location to place significantly more easily than traditional houses.

They can be attractive. Many people like the modern and contemporary appearance of shipping container structures and houses built using shipping containers are simple lines and a modern appearance. The way you finish your shipping container-constructed home they may appear traditional or be decorated with vibrant colours that emphasize the geometric form.

Shipping containers are affordable. The cost of an average shipping container is between $1000-$5000 per container. Based on the way you personalize your shipping container as well as the type of home you're making, this can result in significant savings.

They are extremely tough. They are specifically designed to protect cargo and goods during long sea voyages. They're also waterproof. The strength of their construction makes them a good possibility of lasting for decades as a home with just little maintenance.

They are durable. Shipping containers are constructed of galvanized steel, and are much stronger than wood construction.

They're resistant. Mold and termites are problems in traditional construction but they are not if you build your house using shipping containers. Containers are also highly safe from fire.

Container homes made of shipping containers can be constructed within a relatively short period of period of time. One of the biggest benefits of construction using shipping containers is the short amount of time required to transform the container into a home that is habitable. If you're working yourself or with a team of contractors, you'll discover that the time to construct is drastically diminished. The level of complexity of the design and the amenities you want to put in an empty shipping container could transform into a house within three days.

Shipping containers are good for the environmental. Recycling shipping containers is a great way to make use of shipping containers that could otherwise be rusting in ports across the globe or need to be destroyed in a huge energy consumption.

Why Do We Need Containers?

Although there are a lot of negatives to using container containers, they are numerous reasons you should consider using containers as well.

The concept of making use of prefabricated structures can help you save money on the construction costs. The boxes already have in the proper shape and size for your needs, particularly if you intend to use one. A container that is easily shaped is an economical alternative to the need to construct by hand using conventional construction techniques.

The thousands of container in the globe that are merely standing around and rusting away as they're no longer needed for transportation companies. This is harmful to the environment and is a waste. Wastefulness that is socially acceptable isn't a thing any more. It's green because it's reusing.

The containers that are abandoned are problematic since they occupy space. There is a lot of space actually. There are miles of them because it's expensive for businesses to transport them empty and then wait until they need more cargo to be shipped in that causes them to accumulate in countries which have more imports than exports.

Shipping containers are extremely durable. They're built to withstand the elements of the elements of sun, sea and even travel, so they'll last for an extended period of duration. They're durable and provide a solid foundation for construction projects.

They're a great shape to stack. Like building blocks, shipping containers are large enough to be stackable. Modular designs are simple to build on and are perfect for modular construction.

Their already-made shapes also mean that they're simple to build after they've been delivered, since they're ready-made and don't require a few tweaks.

Container Design Study

Before you design your dream home it's important to know the limits of what you can do using containers. If you're thinking of a small single-container home or a multi-container house These concepts form the basis of how the majority of homes designs are made.

In 1987 the first patent to be granted for the conversion of the shipping container to a dwelling was submitted with Phillip C. Clark. The patent became patentable two years following, as patent number 4855094 should you wish to search for it. The diagrams he created were the basis that architects use today to build these houses. In in 2006 Peter DeMaria designed single-family homes using two containers that were later integrated to the Uniform Building Code in California.

If you're considering plans for any shipping houses I would suggest researching Clark's patent on Google. It's a basic design that eliminates all interior walls, with the exception of two flanges, and it then utilizes a drop ceiling to support the mechanical components. The main difference in Clark's design however is that it does not look like a shipping container. The walls are constructed of exterior materials to disguise the design into what looks like an ordinary home, and you'll be wondering what the purpose of the design was. The reason to look at this particular design is because his patent serves as the foundation of how the majority of container houses are designed even if you're using one container instead two. The window cut-outs along with the elevated floor are nearly identical, even though the design is distinct. This is the most appropriate first step to look at actual designs.

Puma City

The most striking design of all time has to have to be Puma City by Lot-EK. The cost-effectiveness of the design is what has drawn numerous people to the idea of the shipping container design. The design spans three stories tall and contains 11,000 sq ft with two decks and is built with a total of 24 containers. It was awarded the 2009 International Architecture Award, as in addition to numerous magazine awards. It has offices and retail spaces in addition to storage, as well as an open terrace at the top. It is constructed entirely of shipping containers that measure 40 feet and connectors, which are outfitted with covers that cover the exposed areas after the building is removed and then shipped to reconnect the internal spaces. It's revolutionary because it's the first portable shipping container construction.

The issue that is unique about this Puma City building is that it's not designed to be a permanent, habitable residence. It's designed to be an event center which can be assembled and taken apart. Its design is quite innovative, but aside from being an intriguing idea, it's not much more distinctive than the old-fashioned portable office furniture that has been in use for a long time. It's not a permanent dwelling space. The Puma city design is the one you must consider in the event that you are looking to build an easily portable home. It has more than enough space and features the popular modular design, but doesn't require the use of a permanent foundation. Although it may seem expensive for a concept of a mobile home but it's actually a lot larger than a standard caravan.

Mill Junction

Mill Junction was developed by the developer Citiq to provide apartments and facilities to an existing grain silo structure. They were designed to add extra flooring space to existing structures. The idea is one that needs to be considered by those who are looking to build homes using shipping containers but are unsure regarding the viability of constructionIt allows you to retain that classic look however it doesn't limit your options to only using them. In contrast to the hive-inns, this isn't just a concept, it's a real structure located in Johannesburg.

The containers are situated on top and next to the silo's original structure. are the second similar structure to that in the town.

The reason to look at Citiq's design is because you can utilize it to update and improve the structure you have already. A large part of the appeal of shipping containers lies in the aesthetic aspect, not necessarily their physical properties. It is a great idea for those who are trying to create an expansive home since you can use the shipping containers as elements instead of the whole structure that makes it cost-effective and flexible instead of a structure made entirely composed of containers.

The Hive-Inn

OVA studios has come up with this concept for a hotel in a shipping container. The idea is based on the PUMA city-building, but it's not feasible for real housing. It's designed as an elevated structure made consisting of catty-cornered containers that are stacked like an Jenga tower, which is then transformed into an elevated structure. The idea was based on being a building completely flexible, allowing it to be added or removed from anytime. A design like this for a permanent home could be ineffective, especially in the case of cranes and transport costs of transporting and taking containers away, however, on a commercial scale it could be a good idea.

As with the dwell design it's the only thing that you should consider when creating your personal.

The hive is a two-dimensional design of the structure, which are comprised of two containers -those placed side-by-side and those a bit ahead of one another. It is worth looking at this style since it provides two distinct ways to structure the two-container house that is practical and innovative.

We've now looked at commercial developments how do we go about private ones. Private homes must be able to meet different requirements from hotel chains, commercial accommodation or event venues. A home should be a place you can reside in.

Dwell By G-Pod

The idea of dwelling is, however, as feasible as Hive-inn idea isn't feasible. The dwelling concept is thought to be ideal for the case of self-sufficient and transportable houses. It is a mix of pull-out and folding sections to expand the living space in a way that is flexible enough to make it three times the amount of area of the shipping container. It is a great option for those who are looking for green living without the need to hook into water supply lines or an electric grid. Although you might be thinking of the construction of a higher scale, this design could easily be used for human needs.

The concept of the dwell uses slides that cantilever across three different sides of the container which allows the container to "grow" approximately 75 percentage. It means that, while technically using the container as an object, you're not limited by its initial size. This is an innovative method of extending the limits of a tiny box to create the possibility of living in a space that is viable. The other benefit of dwell is that it could be a great idea for those who love the idea of having a shipping container as a home from the standpoint of having a box that is that is with everything already put together.

Pv14 & Manifesto House

If you're looking for more of a luxurious mansion than an eco-friendly home The PV14 home by Matt Moone has an extremely blocky style with a staggering 3700 sq ft of living space. The house is constructed using 14 containers however, like similar to the Mill Junction concept, it includes elements of traditional construction too. It has 3.5 bathrooms as well as a pool. However, it's also packed with other features that create a cozy and luxurious residence. This house is a fantastic option to look at if you're looking for something large modern and contemporary and uses containers as the basis.

Manifesto House is also pretty huge and impressive, but unlike PV14 the emphasis is on recycling, not lavishness. The house makes use of pallets to shield sunlight off the containers. Although this does not allow to view these containers from the outside, it is an inexpensive material for exterior shielding from sunlight. It is also a hugely spacious home, however most of the construction is recycled or green. It is constructed using three shipping containers but includes an exterior space as well as an outdoor balcony. The distinction with this model Manifesto House is that the concentration of the shipping container's design is placed on the inside instead of out. The inside of the walls are clear and unadorned, both on the ceiling and walls and the insulation is completely outside. This allows the container to be properly insulated without compromising the tiny space. It also permits it to maintain the industrial design without completely covering the structure of the container.

Look into manifesto house if you love the concept of a container for shipping but do not like the idea of being constrained by the size because it will provide you with the components you require without being squeezed to squeeze them into a small space.

Chapter 9: How to Build the Home of a Container

Make a list of your top priorities for Your Home

Homes built using shipping containers are growing in popularity as they have for a long time. These kinds of homes offer numerous advantages which make them perfect for those who require an affordable solution for the place they reside. One of these benefits is that they are simple to move and can be moved around to relocate your home quickly when you need to. If you're planning to build or purchase an apartment in a shipping container, this can help you determine the most important things you want to do with your house by determining what kind of items are essential to the home and how much effort needs to be put into each.

Estimate the number of square Feet You'll Be Needing

This calculator is designed to estimate the dimensions of the shipping container. If you are the first time buying containers for your home make sure you purchase the smallest possible size because this is more efficient and will reduce the cost of the project. This calculator is not meant to calculate how much square footage is needed for the finished construction or layout or design.

Find the perfect 20" Shipping Container

If you're like the majority of people who live in shipping containers, then a home built from a container isn't a realistic goal. In the end, how could the humble steel box become the perfect spot to reside?

However, once you look at the idea of homes built from shipping containers, you'll realize that it's not quite absurd at all. Actually, for a lot of people living in rural areas or other countrieshave used shipping containers for a long time as homes!

Zoning & Permits

Zoning regulations are a concern which arises when creating a home in a shipping container. Because of the material utilized, it is important to be aware of whether the location where you plan to build is designated specifically for homes built using shipping containers. To determine this, study the zoning laws of the area where you plan to build.

Generally, urban development areas are generally locations where shipping containers homes are more difficult to construct. As an example, you might require an "variance" regarding the use of shipping containers to be used for residential purposes. You could also encounter opposition from neighbors who are concerned about the impact on their property values the presence of a shipping container in the area will bring. Although the shipping containers are growing in popularity, old-fashioned beliefs persist, along with misperceptions about what a shipping container home should appear like. Making people aware of the benefits of homes made of shipping containers in the area you choose can in reducing this.

Other areas to think about as possible locations for your new home in a shipping container are areas that lie on the edge of rural and industrial zones. In reality, the most suitable site for shipping container homes is to leave the urban limits and into rural zones. Rural areas generally have less restrictions on zoning. However, even with this in mind you must conduct some research. It's not a good idea to buy land to build an shipping container house only and then find out that it isn't possible to build there.

Permits

Additionally, you will need to study the kinds of permits you'll require to get to build your own shipping container home. If you are building it in a location that is suitable for it, you'll need to take into consideration the land rights as well as sewer and water access, as well as other kinds that permit building. State and local governments will be seeking an equal share part of that pie. If you're building your own home it is required to follow the construction regulations of state and municipal governments. Since you're building your own house it is necessary to conduct some additional study. Most builders will be well-versed in codes and permits. As a new builder, must be familiar with these aspects. For this you should talk to local municipal offices, builders in your area as well as the real estate agent. Making the initial research will help you save time and money throughout the process as well as in the long run.

Building Your Dream Home

Before proceeding further with making plans and planning for your home in a shipping container You must determine what your requirements and desires are for a house in addition to the materials you have in your possession.

In this phase it is not necessary to be overly specific in your plans, however you must take the time to note down the number of rooms you'll require, including living space, office space as well as bedroom space. bathrooms and kitchen space. Additionally you'll need to figure out where you will need to reside and where you would like to reside.

Note down the space you believe you'll require and think about mapping it out in your existing home to figure out how big it would actually be. Next, you should determine what kind of financing you could be qualified for and how fast you'll need to have an apartment built.

You might want to consider doing this while studying this book as well as other sources; however, knowing the fundamentals of where the house is located, how large it must be, and the estimated timeframe will aid you in planning your home.

Making a realistic budget

After you've got your plan created, you're ready to start making a budget for your shipping container home. You must create an effective budget in order to manage the costs. If you'd like your house to appear a certain way it is important to do this within a budget that is reasonable for you. Although shipping containers are less expensive than traditional houses, the cost will increase when you don't adhere to the guidelines of a budget. Budgeting can help you make the most value from the construction process, while also saving cash throughout the entire process.

Site Preparation

A home's construction starts with having an area of land where you can build your house. Before you start building your dream home, you will need to determine where you would like to construct it. There are many aspects to take into consideration regarding the location of your container home.

Rust Treatment and Prevention

Rust can be a significant problem for any surface of metal that is exposed to outdoor and water elements. The process of rusting begins by absorbing water into the pores of the metal and is followed by the oxidation of iron. This results in the formation of reddish brown ferric oxide, also referred to as rust. Oxygen, water, and heat trigger this process.

Rust particles attract paints, causing they to shed their protective properties. Rust acts as a catalyst for corrosion of other metals . It could cause structural damage that can lead to malfunction or failure because of weight increases due to corrosion over time.

Commercially-produced products such as galvanizing paint, galvanizing or coatings that contain anti-rust chemicals and recoating may slow down the process of rusting however it's not a solution for the long term.

Rust Removal:

The most effective way to avoid rust is to create the outermost layer from elements. The best preventive measure is to install protective coatings. Those areas that aren't protected with the application of protection must be sanded or bristled to remove particles that are loose, and then apply Rust-X(r) the brand name product, to stop future corrosion. If the rust present has already penetrated into the layer of surface rust there may be a need to eliminate the surface rust in order to obtain the protective coating.

Paint Preparation:

Preparing surfaces for use is the initial step. Rust-X(r) Brand products are not able to stick to rough or oily surfaces, and they will not stick to surfaces treated with oils, waxes or silicone-based cleaning products. Get rid of all dirt, grease or oil and burnt food particles from refrigerators, freezer doors, and ranges prior to painting. Utilize the wire brush or stripping pad to eliminate the surface corrosion. If the rust that is present has penetrated further than the surface layer it is recommended to eliminate all surface rusts in order to build a protective layer.

Rust-X(r) brand products include an oxygen scavenger, which prevents the cold galvanizing reactions that are that are associated with high-risk metals like zinc, from infecting food items or beverages.

Make sure you use the correct paint. Avoid using other coatings, paints or food preparation areas in order to avoid cross-contamination.

Chapter 10: Design Your Shipping Container Home

Inspiration

Small houses are everywhere around us. All over the world containers are being transformed to create private homes. No matter if your thoughts are for an oversized houseboat that can be used as a holiday home, or you've been wanting to construct that treehouse you've had your eye on This article can to start your journey towards a container-based home concept.

Particularly, we will discuss the process that a design firm was able to transform the old container of a shipping vessel into residence that his entire family could live in. It will be clear that the design process involved making changes to the container's design so that it could be more usable and comfortable for the family.

This is an illustration that shows "doing the job yourself" and having lots of fun creating your dream home. It will be clear that containers can be used not just to construct your dream house, but be used as an office at home or even storage shed.

Size and Layout

Please keep these things in mind while designing the Shipping Container home:

* Trailers and trucks should not exceed 24 feet.

* Your home is restricted to a maximum of eight feet wide, however it can be up to 16 feet in length.

The shipping containers should be equipped with a door opening that is at minimum 8 feet from the bottom of its side, and your walkout porch located on the other side.

* You can't over 200 square feet in the total living area (including the floor layout). This is based upon the exterior dimensions of standard-size containers.

Positioning and Orientation

A lot of people don't realize how crucial orientation and location are to the design of homes. Being aware of this aspect is essential to design a practical and visually pleasing living space. In order to have plenty of sunlight entering your home during each day is important to take into consideration the perspectives from different locations.

floor plan and site layout

Containers are available in many shapes and sizes. This is why it's difficult to determine the size and shape the container you choose to use however we'll come up with an approximate idea of floor plans later. The layout will be laid out with a rectangle having about 8 feet of ceiling (2m) to determine the various measurements of each wall

Width of the Container: 2 + 18 inches (1 1/2m) = Width of Side Wall - 1ft (0.3m)

Height of Container: 2 * 8 inches (2m) = the height of Ceiling Wall 1ft (0.3m)

Width of the Room *2 = Width for Each Room - 8 inches (0.2m)

Room Length (Length of the Container 1ft)/2 = length of each Room = 8 inches (0.2m)

Room Width ((Width of the Container) x 18in)/2) Then, divide the result by two. Example: 9ft 9in divided by two equals 4ft 4in, thus that's the length for each room.

In the next step, we'll need to figure out the length the bathroom and hallway are.

The length of the Hallway: (Width of Container - width of the room) + 2 inches (0.5m) is the length of Hallway 6in

Length of the Toilet: This can be determined by adding up the widths and subtracting the size of one doors (1 millimeter).

Size of toilet: 2 - 18-inches = Width the Toilet - 1.25 inches (0.3m)

The next step is to explore different floor plans you could use for containers homes. Remember that this is merely sketchy and should only be used as a rough guideline.

Area Calculations:

Different layouts require different amounts of space. For instance, if intend to build a two bedroom home, the space you require to each room could range from as large as 80 feet. Based on the above measurement and the considerations. Based on the dimensions of your container and the floor plan you'd like to have the size of space needed will vary. We'll look at the different floor plans later and describe the ways they utilize various sizes of space.

A typical home (2 Bedrooms and 1 Bathroom) Utilizes 34 feet (0.36m2) in each bedroom, and 22,4ft2 (0.24m2) for bathrooms and the hallway.

A large home (3 bedrooms and 1 Bathroom) It uses 48ft2 (0.49m2) for each bedroom 22 feet (0.24m2) in the bathroom and 21 feet (0.22m2) to make the hall.

The Final Touch:

After you've decided on the design of your container home it's time to finish it off with some accessories like flooring, ceiling and wall panels that will complete the look.

The most efficient way to go about it is using OSB or plywood panels. OSB panels as they are both cheap and easy to work with. The plywood panels are preferred because they are more robust.

Then, you'll have cut the panels to be sized to each ceiling and wall. The most efficient method for doing this is to use the table saw, but If you're a bit cautious, you could employ a circular saw or handsaw. Each panel's length will be contingent on its width as well as the desired ceiling's height. The size of the panels won't be set, but will determines the height you would like your ceilings. For instance, if the height of your container total is 15 feet (4.5m) high and your ceiling panel's height should be 12 feet (3.6m).

Once you've cut the panels, they'll have to be joined. This can be accomplished with wood screws as well as brackets made of scrap wood. The best option is to use at the very the very least four.

After you've completed the construction of the floors, walls, and ceilings, it's time to think about the possibility of insulation. Of course, the amount of insulation you need will depend on the environment and the amount of heat loss you're anticipating However, if it's an area with cold temperatures, quality insulation is crucial since it will help you save money on cost of energy over the long term.

Topography and Drainage

The container should be able to stand on a level, well-drained area. This means that you'll need an uninvolved hill or a good drainage within the surrounding region. This could also mean moving your landscaping which is far enough from the structure of the new house. Be sure that there aren't any trees that are close enough to put their roots into your foundation in any way.

If you're trying to prevent foundation problems it is not an ideal option. Basements are when the container is placed directly on the ground and water.

To this end, containers are constructed with four walls, and floors made of concrete or wood. This reduces the weight of the bottom of the container , so it won't get sunk easily due to having to hold itself up continuously.

It could be a great idea to create an under-house crawlspace also. This will give plenty of space for shovels, lawnmowers and other equipment you might be using in your yard without exposing them all the humidity that is present below the ground.

A lot of times, the new homeowner may not be aware of how to properly care for this kind of house. It is possible for your container to be soiled and wet particularly in humid regions.

Cleaning out your container on a regular basis is a good idea to keep rot to the low level. After you've taken the container's home it is time to find a location to keep all your items from the house you moved into. Make sure you move into or lease an indoor storage space once you're finished in the box.

Also, ensure you keep accurate records of the materials you move in and out of your new home. A mail-in service could assist in easing any concerns regarding removal of building materials in the future, when it comes time to sell your home.

Access

A shipping container house is an answer to the housing shortage that is afflicting some of the world's most deprived nations. Containers are strong and durable and can be used in a variety of ways. They can be turned into clinics, schools as well as homes. This article we'll look at ideas for designing these containers into houses.

Certain people are drawn to explore more often than they would like to settle in one location Some people want security regardless of where they travel. There are a variety of motives for someone to think about living in containers for shipping and accessibility is one of the main reasons. A lot of people have expressed the desire for living in container homes and a number of cities have implemented strategies to promote this type of lifestyle. Singapore is the home of "cargo villages," or the "cargo village" concept, which includes containers-based homes specifically designed to be sustainable.

Perhaps you're seeking a more remote lifestyle and are looking for a location to store your belongings and ensure your belongings are safe whenever you travel out into the world. There are a variety of options to meet these requirements such as sea-turtle relocation facilities at sea islands and underground storage units as well as space stations. This last option may not be appealing to those who live there, but it might be appealing to other people. Find out more on space stations as well as container homes.

Chapter 11: Ideas of Home Plans Design Your Home

Here are some examples of plans that offer an array of styles.

Examples of Plans

These are only some of the options we have to demonstrate to illustrate the possibilities for customizing the shipping containers homes. Take a look and let the ideas flow!

Plan 1

Plan 1 is perfect for a modest, one-person home. It has the space of 139 square. feet. and is constructed out of a single 20-ft container. It includes a kitchen, dining area as well as a living space and bedroom. The the ultimate in space efficiency and a tiny living space.

Price Range: Less than $15,000

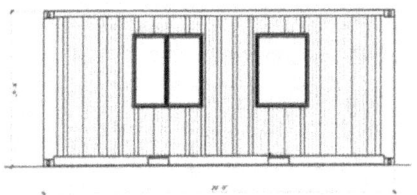

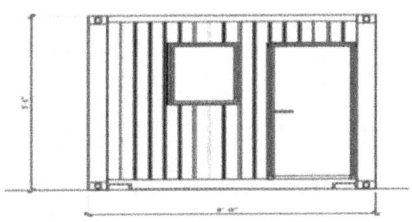

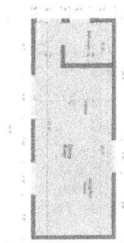

Plan 2

Plan 2 is another example of a single 20-foot container home. It is designed to provide a large kitchen and bathroom. The living space can also be used as a bedroom. It has two double beds that can be pulled out that provide comfort while you are sleeping or sitting. This minimalist design can accommodate two persons within the space of 138 square. ft.

Price Range: Less than $15,000

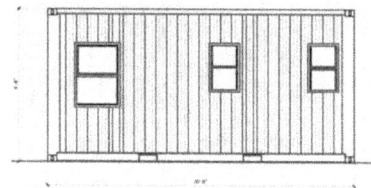

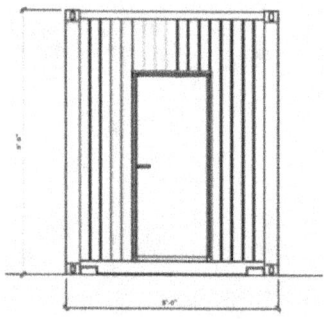

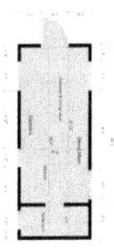

Plan 3

Plan 3 is designed to be an ideal hunting lodge built out of a 20-foot. container. It has a spacious living room that opens up to the kitchenette and bedrooms off towards the back. A deck that is full length runs along across the entire front side of the home which is ideal to relax and take into the night air. It is a spacious space for a one-person home and offers a comfy space for two people if the sofa bed is located in the living area.

Price Range: Less than $15,000

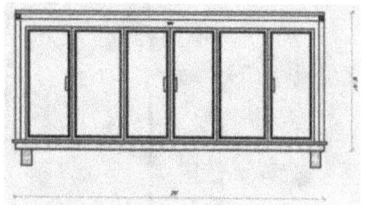

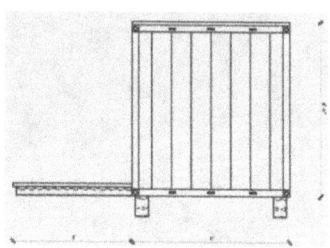

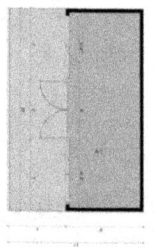

Plan 4

Plan 4 presents a different layout for one 20 feet. container. This style combines space with efficiency, including luxurious bathrooms and a master bedroom with a dining and kitchen. This style is ideal for a single individual or a couple. It offers everything you need to create a wild love nest in 135 square. ft.

Price Range: Less than $15,000

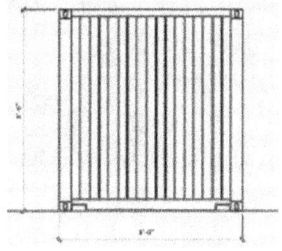

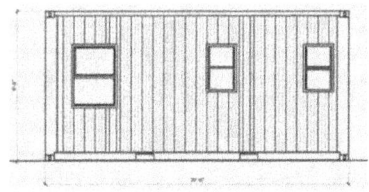

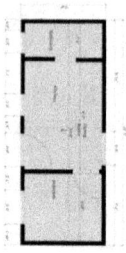

Plan 5

Plan 5 is crafted using one 40-foot. container. It has an open-plan living space that would be perfect for an extra sofa bed. It is equipped with sliding glass doors that lead to a deck that is open. There is also another room, which is perfect as a storage area or as a second bedroom.

Price range: less than $25,000

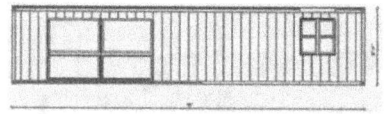

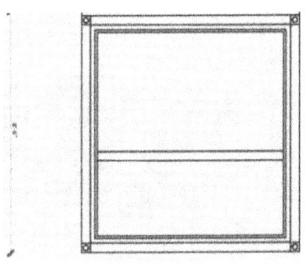

Plan 6

Made out of just a single forty-foot. container Plan 6 offers a amazing 483 square. feet. of living space. It has a living and bedroom room, a spacious dining room, an expansive bath, as well as a comfortable kitchen. This layout is perfect for two persons and can accommodate three or more people with an extra sofa bed.

Price range: less than $25,000

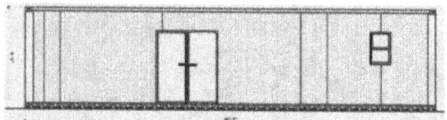

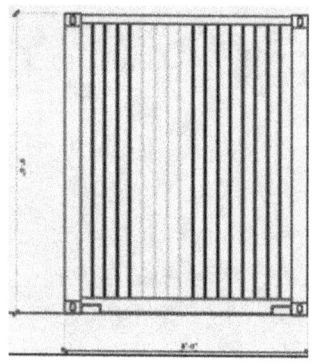

Plan 7

Constructed from only two 20. containers The Plan 7 has 289 square. feet. of living space. The home has the master bedroom, an exquisite bathroom, and a combined kitchen and dining area. The front door is an open-plan living space that is perfect for guests and is furnished with a sofa for a second individual to sleep comfortably.

Price Range: Less than $25,000

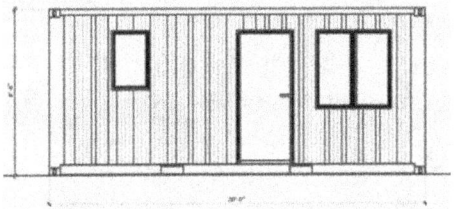

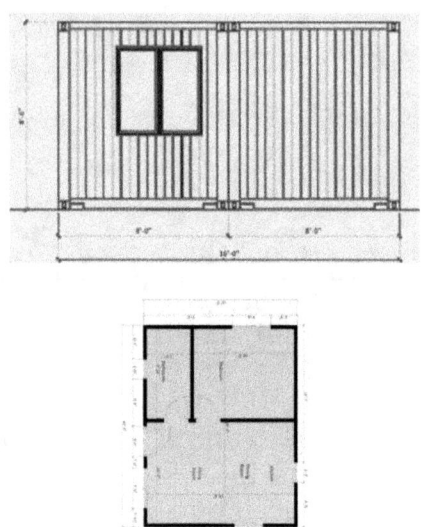

Plan 8

Plan 8 was created with 4 40-ft. container and 4 20-ft. containers. It showcases the luxurious possibilities by constructing homes from shipping containers. The mansion has three bedrooms, two floors as well as three bathrooms. There is also an open-plan living area across both levels. Glass sliding doors at both the front and rear entrances and a deck on the second floor gives this mansion the look of any home built in the traditional style with the utmost decadence.

Price range: less than $35,000

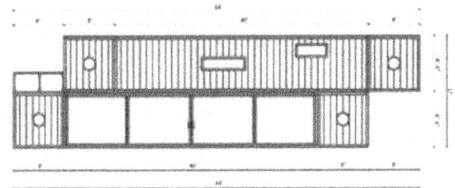

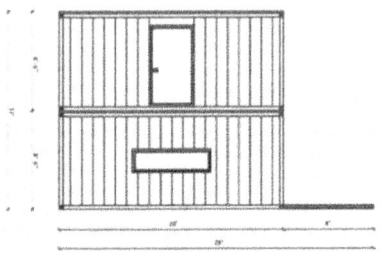

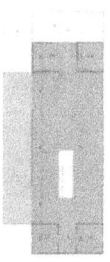

Upstairs:

Plan 9

Plan 9 has three bedrooms and two bathrooms. It also has an open-plan living and dining room. It also has a kitchen, utility room and a closet. There is plenty of space for storage and living in just two 40-foot.
containers. Additionally, there's a deck with a full length that runs on the outside of the home. With 606 square. feet. This house can comfortably accommodate three adults or an entire household of up to four.

Price Range: Less than $35,000

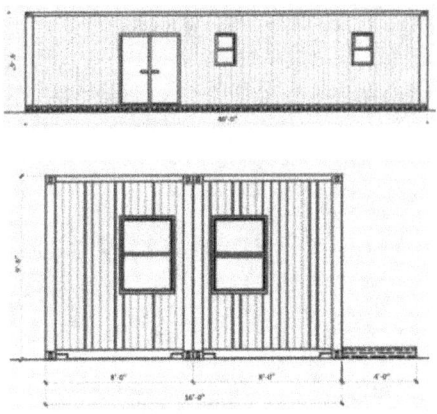

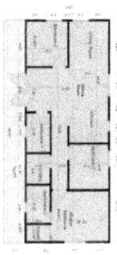

Plan 10

Made of just the three forty-foot. containers and a plan 10 provides a large 899 square. feet. of living space. The home has the master bedroom along with three other bedrooms and two bathrooms. The house also features a designed kitchen, dining room as well as separate living space that is large enough to host guests.

Price range: less than $35,000

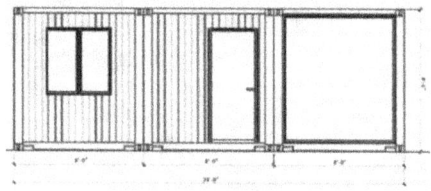

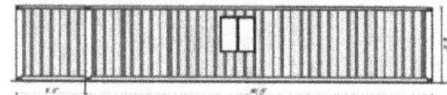

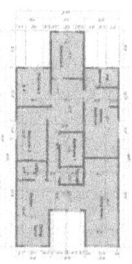

Plan 11

The space is comprised of six 20. container and eight61 square. feet. of living area, Plan 11 offers the highest level of luxury. The upper floor is where you will find three bedrooms as well as two bathrooms. The lower floor is open to living room, dining area as well as a kitchen. There is also the utility closet, which will serve the storage requirements of your home.

Price Range: Below $45,000

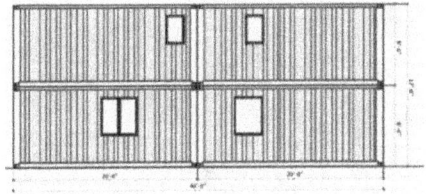

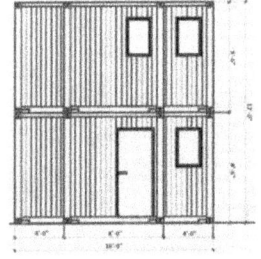

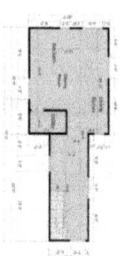

Upstairs:

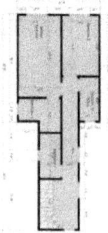

Plan 12

Plan 12 is comprised of five 40-foot. high cubes and offers a total of 1718 square. feet. of living space. It is home to five bedrooms and three bathrooms in addition to a unified dining and kitchen. Additionally, there is the pantry as well as a utility closet. The second floor has an outside deck and terrace ideal for those who want the privacy of the home as well as fresh air.

Price Range: Less than $45,000

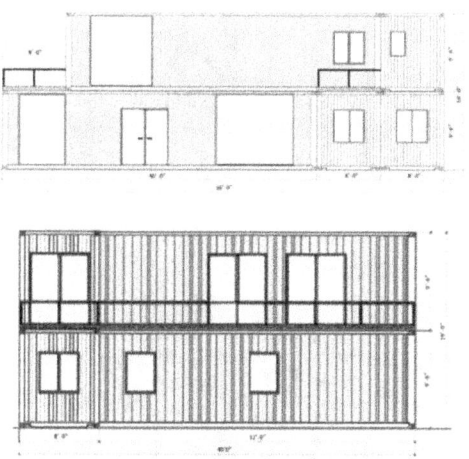

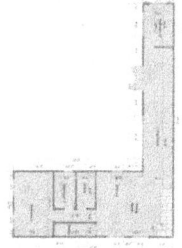

Upstairs:

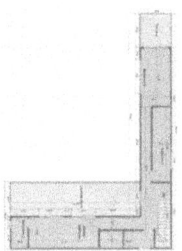

Chapter 12: Preparation of the Site

Marking and Staking

This is a brief overview of steps that I go through to build an apartment in a shipping container. It might not cover everything but it covers the fundamentals and will make you think about what you should take to set up your site prior to the construction.

The first step is to ensure the property has been declared construction sites by the municipal or utility companies, so that they won't charge the cost of any work completed by them. The next step is to mark all the edges of your property as you would do on any typical construction site.

The center line on the bottom of your foundation box using the length of a 4-foot piece of one-inch rebar , pounded to the earth. This is used to locate the center of your structure later. Then, you can lay out the 8' feet wide by the length you require to build the containers frames. Finally, locate any underground utility lines and then mark their locations using a colored spray paint to ensure you don't risk damaging them. The process of bringing in utilities to an existing home is typically more difficult than bringing them into a home which is being built from scratch as the lines are installed which is why it is important to be cautious to not damage them while building.

Grubbing and Clearing

The removal of all trees, shrubs and other vegetation on a property is referred to as clearing and Grubbing. Grubbing also entails taking away roots as well as stumps.

1. Get rid of all vegetation

The grass can be removed by cutting it using the help of a lawnmower, string trimmer or spraying herbicides to destroy the plants. After this, employ a rake to take dirt from the lawn to ensure that the soil is observed. Based on what was sprayed or cut with the string trimmer or lawnmower it is possible that some mulching is required to stop erosion following rainstorms.

2. Drain Water

A drainage trench may be necessary. The trench can be dug using the help of a tube auger or shovel. Be cautious when digging trenches as the soil is usually dry and hard. When there is a root growing in the soil, they could spring up from the soil without warning It is therefore important to dig slow.

3. Eliminating Debris

Trees and stumps that are removed from the ground can result in blood stained sawdust and wood chips, in addition to the remains of nails that fall on the ground. If these materials were stored close to a building in the process of building the new house and must be cleared prior to the beginning of any construction.

4. Make Soil

The soil needs to be prepared to allow for the filling all around the container. The area that is prepared must remain as flat as it can be. This might require an excavation, grading, removal of large rocks, as well as removing tiny roots. Once this is completed the area must be smoothed and any large roots or rocks removed.

5. Use Compost to apply or Mulch

Use compost or mulch to increase the soil's fertility and quality. If compost is used the 4 inch (101 millimeters) of material must be sprayed, and if mulch is used, the 2 inch (51 millimeters) of mulch must be spread."

6. Plant Trees

If planting trees is required then estimate the location of the trees and make the land more livable to make it a good habitat. The trees do not thrive on hard soils. So it is best to prepare the soil to allow them to grow before planting.

7. Graze Hosue Site

After the area has been inhabited for a few months it is recommended that the area be utilized by animals. The grazing process can cause weeds to increase and some of them are required due to the deficiency or soil nutrients. If your home site requires more nitrogen, an andromono-sine-plat could be added

(Aromonosyde Plant). Be aware that plants require lots of sunshine, in addition to enough moisture during their growth.

8. Install Pipes

Once the pipes are put in place, they should be installed in the soil prior to beginning to fill in. If the pipes are put in after filling up the soil, won't bring water to them in a timely manner and may break or leak.

9. Mulch

Place mulch around the pipe prior to filling the pipe with soil.

10. Fill in with soil (Optional)

If there is dirt that has been cleaned off the site of the container, then apply it following the installation the new pipes.

Grading, cutting and Fill

The most important factor to have a successful building experience is planning. It will guide you through the most common aspects of good preparation for your site, and the most suitable levels for your site including hand-dug cuts and fill requirements.

Shipping container homes are built on a flat area of land in order to give the house a more stable appearance. The soil under the container could be graded to ensure the home is well-level. The process of cutting and filling may have to be utilized to ensure that there is enough space beneath the house to store items or for an area for recreation. This is done by digging out dirt and turf from one grass area to fill a different area of grass using dirt or gravel.

Erosion Control

It is essential to prepare the ground to be able to build the foundations of your container home. To ensure stability of your home in the future many issues should be analyzed and addressed.

Erosion control is probably the most important thing to do. If there are roots of plants or underground pipes in the vicinity of the place you're placing concrete in, the concrete could be crushed and could result in costly repairs in the future and the need for repair work following installation. To avoid this, you should place a wire along the edge of the place you plan to build your foundation so you are able to see any hidden objects prior to pouring. This will help you make sure you do not need costly repairs later.

The kind of soil you're dealing with is also a factor. If you're dealing in clay soil, then you'll require an equipment to turn this into sand. This process can cost around $1000 in total expense, however it is highly advised. Concrete will not work on clay because of the amount of water in it. Therefore, you need your house to remain as waterproof as you can. It is preferential to invest the money prior to when the foundation is laid rather than later the foundation is poured, when it will cost you.

The process of pouring concrete over the slope could result in structural problems later on in the future therefore, it should not be done unless it is absolutely required.

There are a variety of different kinds of concrete you can pick from. For a straightforward construction such as the one described here you'll need an easy-setting concrete so that you get your house up as quick as it can be.

To cut costs, make sure that the foundation is being poured simultaneously with the walls of your container. While they are both being constructed, the steel beams are also put in place and this is a option to set your home built quickly. The more complicated your plans become the longer and more budget it will be required to complete them on time.

Road Building

The process of creating roads is a bit complicated and can be completed in various ways. It is all dependent on the requirements and objectives of the construction firm the location, the type of materials, budget, and so on. But, certain steps are typical to all projects regardless of what's been previously mentioned:

Examining the land to build on, and choosing the points for excavation work. Laser measuring or even field measurement.

Excavating foundation trenches for pipes to be installed;

Building access roads to heavy equipment;

Excavating soil in one or more locations in order to construct a the bedding layer

Construction of asphalt surfaces from the top layer of roads (such like bitumen) with lower layers (e.g. stone, sand and crushed rocks) in addition to filling in the soil around the building;

Installation of drainage pipes, sewerage system and electrical system.

Concrete floors are poured, placing bricks or other materials to finish.

Surfaces painted with colors that match to the overall style of architecture;

Fencing and Security

We can provide fencing and security equipment to ensure that your property is secured from possible criminals. We can provide you with a range of options, such as:

Basic Fencing System - Security Fencing Retaining Wall with LED lighting for use at night. Magnets or Electronic Security Gates - CCTV Cameras

Remote Monitoring System to Provide Supervision of the Site

Alarm Systems Phone and email are monitored 24 hours a day by professional trained security personnel in the central office within the UK.

24/7/365 emergency service support available.

Our fence systems are modular, which means they can easily be adapted to meet your fencing needs no matter the size of the property.

Chapter 13: Foundations: Types

Concrete Piers

This is a good option for those who want to save money since it's among the least expensive foundations that are available. It is also easy to put up. The foundation features reinforced steel bars, which serve to reinforce the concrete. Concrete piers are among the most DIY-friendly option, in my opinion. Most often, you'll require six concrete piers per container, two of them in the middle and the remainder used for supporting the corners.

Pile Foundations

Pile foundations are the ones I suggest when you're dealing with a soft soil that is too weak to hold foundations made of concrete. The foundation can be more costly than concrete piers and I wouldn't suggest that you construct this foundation by yourself (unless you're experienced). You'll also require specific tools for this foundation, for instance pile drivers. Your contractor should be able to build this foundation.

Concrete Slab-on-Gram Foundations

The durability of a shipping container's home foundation is among the main features that differentiate it from other kinds of. It is essentially is a concrete reinforced slab that has a steel deck on top. The deck will be connected to walls that are insulated or some other type of raised foundation. It can also be connected to an additional walkway in the middle. This gives the home stability, and protect against wall damage from the inside and also provides protection from noise from outside and drafts. Concrete is not just strong but also extremely robust and simple to fix when required.

If you reside in a region that has an adequate marketplace for shipping containers homes design, you might have seen them built on a slab-on grade foundation. For the home is concerned the foundation and deck are constructed of concrete blocks. They are topped with concrete blocks or cinder block pillars to provide insulation when required. Due to their bulk and size the containers are generally transported via trucks to their destinations and placed directly on the foundation. They can be slid over them in horizontal rows to form the exterior wall of the structure.

The preferred method is also quick however it requires lifting the containers off their trailers and putting them directly onto the spot in the place they are. This is a viable option because of the dimensions of the container and the weight of it. The house itself is constructed using concrete slabs and has interior walls that are made of insulation and drywall, which creates living spaces. The walls inside can reduce outside noise to different levels based on the level you would like your home sounds like. A slab-on-grade foundation can last for for a long time because of this, and its longevity, and is relatively easy to maintain.

Wooden Beams (Railroad Ties)

The shipping container house or a partitioned home is an affordable and sustainable alternative to any type of construction. The homes can be constructed on the top of any foundation, provided that they're sturdy enough. It's usually not difficult to build the components of a container-home in the event that there's enough height between them. The foundation must be sturdy enough, not just to support the container's weight but also the structure as a whole. Another thing to consider is the decision of whether you would like to build storage spaces that are ground-level using this kind of construction style. If you choose to, then you'll require a more sturdy foundation than the one that would typically be built with an elevated floor and storage space design.

In order to build your home it is necessary to figure out how many levels up you want to be. If your foundation is to be placed on the ground it is recommended to use at least 10 tires each 3 inches of height. In the event that the container home you are building is going to be elevated above the ground, you'll require at least 30 railroad tie (or five tires) for each container.

Metal Foundations

The use of containers made of metal to build foundations for houses and buildings. The building components are mainly constructed from metal, and is vulnerable to rust if foundations are not maintained. One possible option could be the shipping container home type of foundation in which containers are used as a structural element for construction. This kind of foundation is a possible solution to the way your existing metal structures can withstand earthquakes while being structurally sound.

It's not new to make use of a cargo container as a structural part. A previous version of this design was developed by Leslie Ekanter where a shipping container was used as the base of his home situated in Sevier, Tennessee. The house was constructed in 2002 and was an uni-story layout featuring two bedrooms as well as a bathroom.

Chemical Contamination

The base of a shipping container for warehouses or shipping container house can be chemically contaminated. Chemical contaminants can vary from paints to plastics and are often caused by inadequate sorting of warehouses that do not have the necessary equipment to sort the contents permanently.

The result is asbestos dust settling in the air above the containers as well as the creation of vents by machinery and pipes that were once within the containers, but are now located outside.

Incredibly, this isn't just an issue for shippers, but also with landlords who have to fill the depots at times with no other option but to lease containers even when they are empty.

The dust is not just an issue in houses however, it is also a problem in the region. The seaports' surroundings, landfills or recycling centers are the most favored areas for contamination of atmosphere and the earth. Asbestos fibers can be easily absorbed by the air and inhaled by people, causing serious health issues due to the carcinogenic character of asbestos.

Chapter 14: things to keep in mind when building a shipping container Home

It's easy to understand why homes built using shipping containers have gained so much popularity. It's all simple enough. All you have to do is purchase one or more containers. They're already made, and each container will be equal to one space. The containers can be stacked together, creating several rooms. If you connect several containers then you will have a larger space. This sounds easy enough, isn't it?

Actually, no. There are a lot of things to take into consideration when using a container for shipping or shipping containers to construct houses. One thing to bear to keep in mind that they were never intended to be used for construction shipping containers; they're cargo containers, and were designed specifically for this. Furthermore, simply being able to use a container isn't enough. It is important to consider things like the HVAC unit, insulation and the list goes on. It is also important to consider that this is an unusual home it is not possible to have any experts to help guide and advise you.

With these in view, we present couple of tips from professionals in the field that deal with shipping containers. These are experts who are either owners or designers of homes like these and the advice they're able to offer is based on the knowledge they've gained by when designing and building these kinds of houses.

1.See Before You Buy

This is the advice offered to Larry Wade. The business you purchase the containers from will assure you, naturally that the containers you purchased are in good shape. However, remember these containers can be designed to move items in all kinds of circumstances, from shaky roadways to rough waters. Although they're designed to last, they are built to stand up to these kinds of conditions, they're capable of beating all the point of being destroyed', as Wade said when he was given his container.

If you consider this, it's the best advice to buy everything. In the case of shipping containers, you should think of this advice as gold.

2. Spend a little extra

As he lamented the condition of the containers he purchased, Larry Wade also wished that he'd paid little more. One-Trip containers are readily available and cost not as much as an used container. The best part is that they're brand new, which means you don't have to be concerned about the condition for the container you purchase. But the first point is valid. Always look over what you are buying prior to actually purchasing it.

3. Learn how to apply the Local Regulations

Of course, this is contingent on the dimensions of the container that you are using. It also is contingent upon what the size minimum needed to be able to get a building permit. Are you able to see what I am talking about? Each county will possess its own set of rules and rules and. If you extend that to state and to the country, things get much more complex.

There is no need to be concerned with council regulations. Different laws govern what constitutes a suitable building material and what's not and who can construct it and the list goes on. The most important thing is to consider various temperatures and patterns of weather. What is effective in Chile for instance, won't necessarily work in Denmark and vice versa.

Find out where you'd like to put your shipping container, and study the local laws and regulations in detail to be aware of what you are allowed and not permitted to do, the permits you will need and so on.

4.Find Someone to take Over All of It

It is crucial to find the right person or business who can guide your through all the steps from beginning to end. That means that the person who the designs and alters the exterior, also takes charge for the inside. It's a concept which makes sense when you consider it. The construction company who builds the shipping container house will be aware of the construction of the house and will be able to integrate designs into the interior which not only compliment the exterior, but also work with it as a structural element.

It also means that you , as the homeowner will not be forced to suffer the burden of recollecting things that you did not even realize you required to remember.

The issue in this particular method is too many companies or people who can assist you. It all depends on where you are as well as your budget as well as other factors.

5.Know about the shipping container Market

Do your research prior to purchasing containers for shipping or a container to build your house. Shipping containers are available in a range of sizes. Check out the different sizes and decide what you require. Explore the market thoroughly and find out what's available and what's not. Do not buy the first thing you see that makes your head clear. Keep in mind that you'll need to install an HVAC system in along with other equipment which will significantly reduce area that needs to be cleared. Think about all this prior to purchasing the container.

6. Understand the structure of Shipping Containers

This is something is not something you can afford to overlook. As I've mentioned earlier it is designed to do just this -- move things around. It's not intended to be used as a construction site. The roofing of the container for shipping is thin and can easily be damaged. The walls of the container serve as braces as well as load bearing structures.

www.ingramcontent.com/pod-product-compliance
Lightning Source LLC
Chambersburg PA
CBHW050409120526
44590CB00015B/1892